UNLEASH THE BEAST

UNLEASH THE BEAST

A JOURNEY TO REDISCOVER
THE GREATNESS WITHIN

Red Letter Publishing, Austin

Unleash the Beast: A Journey to Rediscover the Greatness Within
Copyright © 2016 by Mark D. Rucker
All rights reserved.

No portion of this book may be reproduced, scanned, sold,
or distributed in any printed or electronic form
without the express written permission of the author.

Typeset by Kevin Williamson

Created in the United States of America

22 21 20 19 18 17 16   1 2 3 4 5

ISBN 978-0-9864371-7-5

Dedication

For my wife, Annita. This journey would not have been possible without your constant love and support. And for my children, Mason and Abby, for providing me with the inspiration to change my life.

Acknowledgements

Becoming an Ironman is a lot like raising a child—you need a village to do it. I have had an amazing group of people who helped me along on my journey and for that I am eternally grateful.

I would be remiss if I didn't first thank my parents, John and Jane Rucker, for always encouraging me to march to the beat of my own drum and to believe that I could accomplish anything in this world.

I also need to specifically thank a few people with whom I swam, cycled, and ran countless miles with on this journey, including Ernie Peel, Casey Hill, Leo and Mona Brown, Katie Cloninger, Bill Cole, Fran Bevins, Tom Walters, Laurie Roberts, Jen Connors, Coy Martinez, and Jill Kimberlin. I also need to thank all of the members of the Bluegrass Cycling Club, Bluegrass Triathlon Club, and the UK Masters Swim Team.

I would also like to acknowledge my amazing coaches who guided me, encouraged me, and kicked my butt along the way to get me across the finish line— Susan Bradley-Cox and Beth Atnip.

Finally, I need to thank my writing coach, Cathy Fyock, for all of her guidance with this book, as well as my editor, Kevin Williamson, and all of the folks at Red Letter Publishing.

INTRODUCTION
1
DESIRE
5
INSPIRATION
19
VISION
29
KNOWLEDGE
43
BELIEF
53
DETERMINATION
65
CONCLUSION
75
PHOTOS
79

INTRODUCTION

I'll never forget the bus ride back from LaGrange to downtown Louisville in 2012. I can still feel the hot summer air blowing from the open window a few seats in front of me. I can recall the constant chatter from the other people riding the bus with me that day. I can still smell the diesel fumes from the engine.

Thinking back on it now, I couldn't tell you a single thing about any of the people with me—who they were, what their names were, where they were from. I knew one thing about them all—actually, about all of us, myself included. I knew where we were headed and I knew why. On that hot August day, we were headed back to the drop-off point for drop-outs of Ironman Louisville.

I felt like a loser, a failure. My family and friends were waiting for me. I was so embarrassed—how could I face my wife? My friends? All the people who had supported me over the past 18 months? Even worse, how could I face the people who had doubted me? Now they could say that they'd been right, that I wouldn't be able to do it, to achieve my dream of being an Ironman. They were right and I was wrong.

That was the longest bus ride of my life.

Once I made it back to the drop-off point, my wife and friends were there. There was none of the gloom; they were smiling and cheering and supporting me anyway. At the time, that was what I needed to feel better. But it wasn't enough. I still felt like a failure—and it was a terrible feeling I couldn't shake.

And over the next few months, I struggled tremendously to find the drive to get back on track. I fell back into some of my old, bad habits. My thoughts became cloudy, negative, and gray more often. Worst of all, the weight I'd worked so hard to lose, in my transformation from couch potato to Ironman, had slowly begun to creep back onto my body.

I'd been down this road before, and more times than I'd like to admit. *Change my eating habits. Change my exercise habits. Stick to it. Do great.* And then—*derail*. Go back to the old ways; gain back all the lost weight and even more. It was already an old story for me, and I feared I was about to lose *all* of the tremendous gains that I'd made over the past 18 months.

But not this time. No. It didn't happen. This time, things were different; *I* was different, and my entire approach to life was different. I had developed a method to achieve success, and I was determined to see my dream become my reality. Twelve months later, I did achieve that dream when I crossed the finish line at Ironman Louisville. I heard the Ironman announcer shout, *Mark Rucker, you are an Ironman!* It was one of the greatest moments of my life, and I won't forget it as long as I live.

And now, I want to share the reason for my success with you.

* * * * *

Do you ever think back to when you were a child? Do you remember the carefree attitude that you had? *No worries. No stress. No responsibilities.*

Do you remember thinking about what your life would be like when you grew up? What you'd be? Who you'd marry? How wonderful it'd all be?

Do you remember when those dreams slipped away?

I certainly don't. I dreamed of being an Air Force pilot. I dreamed of flying amazing planes really, *really* fast. But, over time, that dream faded. Thinking back on it now, there was no exact moment in my life when that dream faded; it just did, over time, slipping through my hands like water.

And over time, as life threw me more and more curveballs, I seemed to get farther and farther off course. It wasn't any one big change that sent me awry; it was just the sum of years of small adjustments until one day, in February 2011, I woke up at the age of 42 weighing almost 400 pounds and afflicted with a number of health problems.

My life looked *nothing* like the dreams from my youth. The time I'd lived was lost and gone, and I didn't remember how I had gotten to that point. But I knew that I needed to make a change—and so I did.

I have a feeling that you may be at that point in your own life. You may think to yourself, as I once did: *how did I get here?* Maybe even: *Who have I allowed myself to become?*

And you know what? It's okay. It's *okay* that you're at that point, that you are where you are. We all come to moments like these, and we all ask those same questions. It may not be your health; it may be your job, or your finances, or your relationships. Whichever part of life is in tumult, you might feel a sense of despair about it.

But I have some great news for you.

You have made the decision to make a change. You have taken that first small step on a new journey. On your own power, you purchased this book and you're reading it right now. In doing so, you are trying to steer your ship back on course, and that's exactly what this book intends to help you do.

I'm not saying that you'll be back on course in a matter of days, weeks, or even months. This book isn't a scheduled program; what you need for yourself may take a year or two to accomplish. It took me four—but I did it. Along the way, I learned what I now call the Six Building Blocks of Success to help myself; apply them for yourself and you will achieve that dream that you thought had passed you by.

So congratulations on getting started—and now, let's begin the journey to rediscover the greatness within *you*!

CHAPTER ONE
DESIRE

> *"When your desires are strong enough, you will appear to possess superhuman powers to achieve."*
> — *Napoleon Hill* —

Allow yourself to think about *superhuman powers* for a moment.

As a child I was fascinated with superheroes. Of all the superheroes, Spiderman was my favorite, I think because, when he wasn't Spiderman, he was Peter Parker—a normal, guy-next-door type. There wasn't anything amazing about him as an ordinary person; once there was trouble, though, he *did* become amazing. Hence, of course, "the Amazing Spiderman."

He could swing from strands of web aimed from his own wrists. He could climb up sheer walls and along ceilings. He could scale buildings from top to bottom with no trouble. It didn't hurt that he was super-strong as well. I wanted all of those powers; who wouldn't?

Who was *your* favorite superhero? My guess is, whoever it was, it was most likely because of the powers that particular superhero possessed and that, if you could choose, you'd have similar superpowers for yourself. Here we return to Mr. Hill's wisdom: when your desires are strong enough, you *do* possess superpowers. Perhaps not Superman's power of flight or Wonder Woman's magic lasso, but you *will* possess the power within you to change any aspect of your life that you decide to change, whether it's your health, your fitness, your finances, your job, or your relationships.

It sounds easy, right? If you truly desire a change in your life, and strongly enough, then it will happen based on that desire. That's that, right?

Wrong!

Desire is the first Building Block of Success, and the first block in the Dream Stage (more on that later). There are five other Building Blocks, as there's a good deal more to consider after Desire—still, it's an important starting point for achieving the success you desire, so let's examine it in more detail.

Where Does Desire Come From?

Desire is both a noun and a verb. However, when I discuss Desire as a Building Block of Success, I am referring to its verb form. *Desire* is a word of action. It means "to long or hope for."

The desire to change for each person is unique to that person. It may be triggered by an event that happens in your life, or perhaps from something that you read, or a conversation that you have with someone. My point is that the desire to change your life can be triggered by anything.

In my case, the desire to change my life was triggered by a family vacation to Gatlinburg in June of 2010.

We planned our week so that the day at Dollywood would be our final vacation activity. After patiently waiting all week long for it, our big day finally arrived and my daughter, Abby, was so excited to get there. We were (nearly) the first people at the park, and we waited, rather impatiently, for the workers to open their windows and start taking our tickets. It seemed like hours just standing there waiting for our chance to get into the park, but it gave my daughter and I time to plan how we could be the first ones to the rollercoaster. Once they let us in, my daughter and I were off to the Thunderhead.

I wasn't in the best of shape, and the walk to the coaster, even though it wasn't that far, was such a struggle for me. It was the middle of the summer, and even though it was only 9 a.m. it was already hot and muggy. I began sweating and breathing heavily as we made our way back and forth on the winding black walkway to the coaster. To me, it seemed like every step was uphill; I had to stop several times on the way. I acted like I was looking at different things along the path so no one would know that I was winded, but I needed to catch my breath. *I was so out of shape.*

Eventually we made it to the ride and we got in line. Unfortunately, because of my rest stops along the way, we weren't at the front of the line (we weren't even close). But that was okay, because after waiting all week for this moment to arrive, we had finally made it! We were in line for the scariest roller coaster in the park; we heard the screams of terror and excitement from the people riding before us as the big wooden coaster clicked and clacked its way over the wooden boards. I was thrilled to finally share something that I'd enjoyed so much with my daughter, and I could tell she was just as excited.

Finally it was our turn. We had positioned ourselves toward the back of the ride (because everybody knows that's the best place to sit on a rollercoaster). As the two previous riders got out of our car, we stepped in. My daughter was small enough that we were able to fit together comfortably side by side; she was fine in about half of one seat while I took up the remaining seat and a half. Regardless, we were ready to go.

I reached down to grab the safety belt and quickly strapped us in. *It was almost go time.* My daughter and I were both nervous and excited, and we were laughing to ourselves about the terror that was waiting around the corner.

I reached over my head and grabbed the safety bar; I pulled it down to lock it into place, but before I was able to get it clicked into place, it stopped. It was stuck against the top of my stomach. Try as I might, it just wouldn't go down any farther.

I adjusted myself in the seat and sat up a little taller, then pushed again. *No luck.*

I sucked everything in the best that I could and gave it another go. Still no luck. I laughed nervously while looking at my daughter, saying something about how they *really* wanted to make sure that we wouldn't fall out. I was trying to reassure her. And although I was still laughing on the outside, I was really starting to worry on the inside.

A part of me already knew. *I'm not going to fit.*

By this time, all of the other riders were strapped down, locked into place, and ready to go. I was holding up the ride at this point; everyone else was ready to have their fun. Unfortunately, me and my 385 pounds were in the way—literally and figuratively.

The two attendants working the ride came back to me and gave me some advice on how to adjust myself in order to get the bar locked into place. I did everything they said; I sat up as tall as I could, I wiggled this way and that, I sucked in my gut like I was trying to squeeze out the only exit of a sinkhole. Both attendants gave the safety bar a push, then another and another. They pushed so much that my stomach was starting to hurt from the bar being pushed against it.

Once they'd tried, the attendants looked at me and just said, "Sorry, sir, you won't be able to ride today." The humiliation and embarrassment I felt was overwhelming. It felt to me like hundreds of eyes were touching me, that *everyone* nearby was watching this scene unfold. I knew what they were all thinking to themselves: *That guy's too fat to ride the roller coaster. Bummer.*

My daughter and I stepped out of the car. However excited we'd been, we wouldn't be riding it together that day.

I knew then that I needed to make some significant changes in my life. That day, I promised my daughter that I would make those changes and that we would return and ride those rides together.

But I didn't make those changes all as I had promised. I had the *desire* to change, but following through was something completely different. The first Building Block of Success was in place, but the other five were still missing.

The Difference Between Desire, Wants, and Passion

When you think about that particular aspect of your life that you would like to change, is it something that you long for? I think there is a big difference between the Desire of our lives and what we *want*.

Here's what I mean. I often catch myself saying things like *I wish I had that new car* or *I wish I had that fancy gadget*. Most of us are wired that way; we see things every day that we would like to have, or we see people living a certain lifestyle and we think, "You know, I would love to have that life."

Does that mean that those are our Desires? No.

I knew that changing my life was more than something I merely wanted. After the trip to Gatlinburg, it was something that weighed heavily on my mind every single day. Even when I'd try to push away my thoughts about losing weight and being healthy, they would always creep back into my mind. I knew that this was something much more than an empty wish; it had become something that I truly *desired*. And although I didn't know how to make it happen, the Desire stayed with me and intensified in the months after the vacation.

If there is a part of your life where change needs to be made, and it's something that you think about on a regular basis, you're beyond the "wanting and wishing" phase. Congratulations again—you have now laid the first Building Block of Success, Desire. As we move through the following chapters, I will show you how to continue to build on your Desire so you can achieve your own success.

There is also a difference between desires of this kind and passions. I have many different passions: my passion for music, my passion for service and helping others, my passion for inspiring myself and others, and so on. Most of us have different passions in our lives, but being passionate about something isn't the same as saying that thing is your Desire.

Of course, it's possible that your passions and your Desire can line up. It's just important to realize that they aren't necessarily the same thing. It's a Desire I had to lose weight and be healthy; it wasn't merely something that I felt *passionate* about. Now that I have achieved my success in being healthy, I am able to use the principles that I developed for myself to help others change aspects of their lives. (There's that passion for service and inspiration.)

People need to be passionate; it's a good trait. I encourage you to find areas in your life where you exhibit passion and to share that passion with others. If that passion aligns with your Desire, by all means pursue it; as you develop the other

Building Blocks of Success you will be able to bind your passions and Desire together to achieve your success.

As I write this book, my new Desire is to be an author and speaker. I want to share my health and fitness journey, and the principles that I developed, with as many people as I can. So my Dream of being an author and speaker is—to me, now—the perfect combination of my Desire to write and speak and my passions to help others and change lives.

The Stages of Desire

Now that you've identified your Desire, it's important to understand the stages of Desire. As you move through the six Building Blocks of Success, your Desire will evolve in three stages along the course to your ultimate success. I call these-stages the *ABCs of Desire*.

The first level is the *actualizing stage* of Desire, where wants and wishes are filtered and you can realize, with clarity, what you truly want the most. You have made your wants or wishes into something actual; they are now your Desire. This is the period where you're likely to think about this change constantly and, regardless of what you might do to block it out of your mind, it somehow manages to creep back in.

Each person will move through the three stages at their own pace. For me, the actualizing stage of Desire lasted for almost seven months. I knew that I wanted to change my life, but I didn't take any deliberate action toward the success I wanted. (It took learning the Second Building Block of Success before I was able to move into the next stage of Desire.)

The *building stage* of Desire is the second. We will discuss this more as we move into the next few chapters, but for now, what's important is to understand that you will need to incorporate additional Building Blocks of Success to move into the building stage of Desire. This stage of Desire is where your Desire takes on intentional actions for achieving the success you want. Your Desire intensifies and grows even stronger at this point. It may even become your main focus each day.

The third and final stage of Desire is the *completion stage* of Desire. In this final stage, you move closer to the ultimate success that you seek and eventually achieve that success. At this stage, your Desire has become the force that drives you daily; your actions are focused on reaching your ultimate goal and you are determined, so much that you can't imagine *not* being determined.

On my journey, my Desire to lose weight intensified significantly as I moved through the three stages of Desire and incorporated additional Building Blocks of Success. When I started my journey, I began by eating healthy and walking. As I progressed in my Desire to be healthy, I stopped walking and started running.

I started with the modest goal of completing a 5K. And after training for 9 weeks, I did successfully complete my first 5K. I kept training and went on to complete a 10K, then a half-marathon, then a full marathon. I did all of this within 12 months of making the decision to change my life.

But I didn't stop there. I included swimming and cycling into my exercise routine and began training for the Ironman. Although it took me an extra 18 months to achieve the dream of becoming an Ironman, become an Ironman I did.

What started out in March 2011 as 30 minutes of walking three times a week evolved over time—as I moved through the three stages of Desire—to become over 20 hours of running, swimming, and cycling each week.

Now I'm not saying that each of you will be able to spend 20 hours per week focused specifically on your Dream, but as you move through the three stages of Desire, you will notice that you devote more and more time to achieving your success. As you incorporate the other Building Blocks of Success, you will move through this progression quite naturally, and before long you will be amazed at what you are able to achieve on your own power.

It's important to understand that there is no quantifiable measure of Desire. As you move through these levels, it will be a unique experience for you and each other reader. It might be easier if you could somehow take a measurement and say "Yep, I've entered the building level of Desire," but unfortunately it's not so cut-and-dry (nothing's simple, right?).

As I mentioned earlier, each level of Desire will become visible to you as you incorporate more of the Building Blocks of Success into your journey. As you find yourself regularly thinking about a change in your life, to the point that you can't put it out of your mind even when you try, you know you've entered the actualization level of Desire. It may take you a few weeks; it may take you seven months, as it did for me.

As you incorporate more of the Building Blocks of Success into your journey, you will enter the building stage of Desire. Again, there will be no specific indicator that you've reached this level, but once your Desire becomes part of your daily thought process and you begin taking regular actions toward making your Desire your reality, then you've entered the second level of Desire. Again, there is no time limit here. But once you get closer to your goal, you will enter the *completing stage* of Desire. At this point, your Desire has become the primary driver of your day-to-day life. You are completing the small, incremental goals that you have set and you are determined to achieve your Dream. This final Level culminates with achieving your Dream.

Cultivating Desire Through Numbers

I wrote earlier that Desire is unique to each individual and I firmly believe that. The ABCs of Desire will be a journey that each individual will make at his or her own pace. It is part of the process of achieving your success. However, I do believe that there is great value in cultivating your Desire by interacting with other like-minded individuals—it could be anything from a Facebook group to a group of friends to a support group, anything that allows you to interact with others in a way that supports your Desire.

When I started my health and fitness journey, I shared almost everything I did on Facebook. It was a way for me to maintain a level of accountability, but it also allowed me to share my experience with others and find other people who were also thinking about losing weight and getting healthy. As I progressed in my journey, I found more and more people who shared my Desire, and we were able to encourage and support one another. The more I talked to others about my Dream, the more I wanted it, and the better-equipped I was to reach it.

It's important to point out that the Desires of other people don't have to be exactly the same as yours. You might want to achieve total financial freedom while someone else just wants to pay off a few bills—but each of you want to improve your financial situation, so there is enough similarity in Desire that it can be a benefit to support one another.

My half-marathon training is a perfect example. As I moved from walking to running, I did all of my running by myself. I was very slow and was always very self-conscious of what others might think of my running ability (or lack thereof). After I finished my 10K and moved into half-marathon training, I realized that I would need the support of other people. For that reason, I joined a local running group and found an incredible amount of support from other people training to run a half-marathon.

At that point, my Dream was to lose over 100 pounds and become fully fit and healthy. That was my ultimate Desire. Along the way, though, I had to set small, incremental goals to reach that final destination; running a half-marathon was one of those incremental goals. Having other people with the same goal, running the half-marathon, helped align me with the support I needed to stay on track.

Your Desire might be something completely different from my own. You may Desire to improve your financial situation, or your career, or even your relationships. I highly recommend finding a group of like-minded people to help you strengthen your Desire. You can find a group of people for most sorts of goals and Desires you can have; for example, if you wanted to improve your personal financial situation, you could look into joining a Dave Ramsey "Financial Peace" small group. Whatever area of your life you want to change, you can find help through others experiencing similar challenges.

I will include a caveat here, though. While being involved with others may help strengthen your Desire, don't let the Desires of other people displace your own. It can be easy sometimes to fall into the traps of groupthink, when a group of people work together and over time their individual, disparate wants are replaced by the group's wants. It can be an easy trap to fall into, so make sure that, as you work with others, you always evaluate your Desire and whether the group is helping you to strengthen that Desire for yourself—or not. If you find that your Desire has somehow been replaced with someone else's, it's time for you to re-define what you want to achieve with your association with the group. If you can't achieve that in the group, it's time for you to leave.

This happened for me with my running group. As I continued to progress through my training, I eventually transitioned into triathlon training, and so I began to focus on swimming and cycling in addition to running. Nobody else in my running group had that Desire to become an Ironman. At times, there were members of the group who questioned my decision to train for Ironman and actually questioned whether I would be successful in achieving that goal. I knew then that staying with the group would become more of a hindrance to my success—so I made the difficult decision to leave the group. I lost some friends as a result of my choice. The exact same thing may happen to you on your journey, but you must realize that true success requires these difficult breaks and decisions.

How To Handle Declining Desire

Yes. Despite all I've been saying, about how my Desire was often rising, you may find it sometimes *decreases* during the course of your journey. It doesn't mean that you're on the wrong path or that you're pursuing the wrong things. These can be very natural parts of achieving your success. What's important is being able to identify the difference between a typical lull and a true change in your Desire.

Most of us are wired to believe that, when we pursue a dream, we have to give it 110% all the time. This is true much of the time, but there are some occasions when it's important to step back and check yourself again. That doesn't have to mean that you've been wasting your time, or that you're going to have to give up. It simply means that some adjustments are needed, or maybe even a break; in my case, a reminder was due that muscles grow by being destroyed and then coming back stronger. Sometimes rest, not more work, is what you need to move forward and come back stronger.

A waning of your Desire can occur at any point along the way, and at any of the three stages of Desire. It's important to evaluate the significance, though, at each of the three Stages to determine the impact that it may have on your path to achieving success.

At the *actualizing stage* of Desire, you have only just made the transition from wish and want to something more concrete. You have achieved the first Building Block of Success and your journey is just beginning. If you find that your Desire is already declining at this point, it may be a strong indicator that your Desire was, in fact, nothing more than a wish that intensified for a brief period of time. It's essential, at this point, to do some soul-searching and decide if this is truly your Desire or not. It's far better to make the decision carefully at this stage of the process—the earlier you make this decision, the earlier you can redirect yourself towards what you *do* want if what you want isn't along this path. You might waste a lot of time and trouble otherwise.

You might even want to just take some time and back away from everything for a few days. If you find that it's easy for you to stop thinking about your Desire after a few days, that you're at peace with it, then it's safe to say it wasn't something you truly desired. The important thing to realize is that it's okay to make that decision. It's a smart decision, actually.

Here's the other possibility, though, and the one most worth considering: if you back away from things and then you *still* continue thinking about them, that you feel uneasy about backing away from them, you probably do want it—and I would encourage you to pursue it. As you develop the additional Building Blocks of Success, you will become more focused in your Desire and realize that you made the right choice to pursue it.

If you find that your Desire declines during the building Stage of Desire, more likely than not it's a temporary decline. Taking a few days or weeks (or even months) away from your efforts may be just what you need. I know it may sound strange to advise taking several months off, but it can work. You come back a different person, and that break may be *exactly* what you need to help you refocus and even redefine your Desire.

When I attempted Ironman Louisville in 2012, I felt like I was ready to achieve my Dream of being an Ironman. I had trained very, very hard and was dedicated hard as iron to making it happen. When I had to drop out of the race at Mile 48, I was devastated. I felt like I had let down my friends and family; I felt like a failure. I talked about coming back the next year to finish it, but there was a part of me that questioned whether or not I could achieve my Dream at all.

Over the next few months, after Ironman Louisville, I took several months off. I ran sparingly. I cycled only a few times with friends. I swam once or twice. I even let my nutrition slip and I fell back into some old habits. I really wasn't sure, during that period, whether training and competing in Ironman was something that I really wanted to do again. It would take a lot of time and effort and money—again. I honestly didn't know if I could do it.

But as time passed, I felt a sense of emptiness. I thought about Ironman every day. Even after months, I felt guilty for not training. I felt like I was letting *more* people down by not continuing than I had by not finishing the Ironman in the first place. As I thought about it, I realized that being an Ironman really had been my Dream. It *was* my Desire. It was something that I *needed* to achieve, or I wouldn't be able to rest. And so, after taking five months off from a consistent schedule of training, I finally got back with the program. When I went back in 2013, it ended with me achieving my Dream.

If the decline in Desire happens to you during the completing Stage of Desire, you don't need to consider quitting. You will face a decline at some point during this period. It's normal. Begin with the thought that all declines are temporary, and they are; but if you see a dip and decide you're going to quit, it would be catastrophic. You've invested too much time and effort at this point to stop—so don't.

When I started training again for Ironman Louisville 2013, I knew that I had made the right choice. I hired a coach and began full-time training in February 2013. The race was scheduled for August 25th—six months to prepare.

My training went really well for the most part. My coach lived in Colorado, but we used an online training program and, each Sunday, she would upload my workouts for the week. I'm a "check off the box" kind of guy, so I got a great sense of accomplishment checking off each swim, bike, and run as I completed it.

Then life did what it likes to: it threw me a curveball. My wife's mother had been battling dementia for a couple of years and was descending into Alzheimer's. She had her good days and her bad days. My wife was very close with her mother, so to see her spiraling took a real toll on my wife. In turn, it took a major toll on me. I'd never felt so helpless. I love to fix problems; I think most men are wired that way. But this was, of course, a problem that I couldn't fix. In April, we found out that my mother-in-law had cancer too.

No one saw it coming. She'd had some pain and stomach issues, so my wife took her to the doctor for a check-up. The result of the doctor's visit was a Stage-4 cancer diagnosis. My wife and I were a train wreck.

Six weeks later, in early June, we lost her. We were there by her bedside as she took her last breaths. It was so difficult for us, but we knew at least that she was no longer in pain.

The few weeks after the funeral were something of a blur. I trained when I could, but I wanted to be there for my wife as much as I could spare. My training schedule was already demanding about 15 hours per week, on top of a full-time job as an attorney. To say it was tough doesn't say enough; by July I couldn't do it anymore.

I remember calling my wife one day in July, just a little over a month before the race, to tell her that it was over. I was finished. I wasn't going to do it. I had lost my focus and just didn't feel I could regain the strength that I needed. I felt hollow. I knew she was devastated. She told me later that, when she hung up the phone, she sat in her car and cried for almost an hour.

Once we were both at home, we discussed it in more detail. She told me that my decision didn't just affect me; it affected her, my kids, my friends, and every person out there who believed in me and *wanted* to see me cross that finish line. Her words hit home with me. I decided then that I would finish my training, that I would do my best to finish the race.

So again let me warn you: you will experience a decline in your Desire. Life events might sidetrack you. Maybe you hit a wall and need a break. Whatever the reason when it comes, it's important to understand that it *will* happen at some point. Just don't let it derail you. Stay focused; stay determined. Let your Desire lead you even when you don't feel it should be allowed to.

Now that we've determined that you have a Desire to change your life, our next chapter will outline the next Building Block of Success. I will share the principle of Inspiration with you; we will discuss how Inspiration combines with Desire to drive you forward on your journey to success.

CHAPTER TWO
INSPIRATION

"Genius is 1% inspiration and 99% perspiration."
— *Thomas Edison* —

While I'm not usually one to argue with a man as smart as Edison, I do think Edison may have been just a *little* bit off in his calculation. In my book, success requires more than just one percent inspiration. It is the second Building Block of Success, and through this chapter we will delve into Inspiration much deeper than our friend Mr. Edison may think it worthy.

Where Does Inspiration Come From?

Inspiration can come from many, many places. Some inspiration comes from music, others from a beautiful sunset or an inspirational example. It doesn't much matter where the inspiration comes from; much like the First Building Block of Success, Desire, Inspiration is unique to the individual. What inspires me may not necessarily inspire you and vice versa.

Inspiration means "being mentally stimulated to do or feel something." If we break that definition down, we see that inspiration is basically comprised of a mental aspect and a physical aspect. When we are inspired, our minds are stimulated by the person, event, or thing and that stimulation, in turn, leads us to the real and physical aspect of taking some sort of action.

So the Inspiration to change your life may come from a completely different place than they do for everybody else, but that doesn't matter. Inspiration is unique to you. If you find something inspiring, it's inspiring, and there isn't much need to explain it.

My inspiration to change my life came from another person, a friend of mine whom I had known since I was six years old. Anita Holbrook Mills and I went to school together and even played little league baseball together. We weren't *close* friends in high school, but we knew each other well enough and did consider one another friends. After high school we lost touch and rarely saw one another.

Like many high school friends, our interaction was limited to the five-, ten-, or fifteen-year reunions. But through the magic of Facebook, we reconnected in 2009 for a short time—then she seemed to disappear from Facebook altogether, at least until later in 2010.

I should mention: much as I did, Anita struggled with her weight throughout school. But when Anita reappeared in 2010, she looked like a completely different person. Anita had lost *a hundred and eighty pounds* through diet and exercise! I was absolutely amazed. And it couldn't have happened at a better time; this was just after the trip to Dollywood where I was too big to fit on the roller coaster with my daughter. That trip had created my Desire for change, but I had never taken any steps toward making those changes. Anita's story captivated me and I wanted to know more.

Once she was back, I spent a lot of time talking with Anita on Facebook about what she had done and how she had managed to change her health. She had developed a simple plan with the help of her doctor, then she managed to lose the 180 pounds over the course of a year. She looked great, and she said that she felt great. I wanted that for myself—badly. In turn, I Desired it. With her example in my mind, now I had the Inspiration to make it happen.

Anita and I continue to stay in touch; she ending up losing a total of 242 pounds. Her story was featured in *Women's Day Magazine* and on *The Rachel Ray Show* and *The Today Show*. I credit Anita with providing me with the Inspiration that I needed to move my Desire to something more powerful, and I am forever thankful to her for sharing her story with me and so many others.

Having told you about Anita, I will say: just because my Inspiration came from another person doesn't mean that your Inspiration will necessarily come from another person. I hope that many of you find my story inspiring, that it might serve as your source of Inspiration—but if not, your Inspiration is out there.

The Difference Between Inspiration and Motivation

As we mentioned earlier, Inspiration has a mental aspect and a physical aspect; a mental stimulation leads to a physical response, and how that is wired is unique to each person. What inspires you may not inspire someone else.

Like Inspiration, motivation involves a mental stimulus of some form; when someone says that they are motivated to do something, it means that they have thought about it and are prepared to act on it.

Motivation is something that drives you to act in a specific way toward a specific result. Motivation is fleeting; if the need disappears, so does the motivation. Inspiration, on the other hand, is constant; it changes your thought process more permanently; it has its way of staying with you, and it can drive you in ways that fit you and your unique goal.

When a coach tries to fire up her team prior to a game, the goal is to motivate each member to play her best and to win the game. There is a mental stimulus (the coach's pep talk) that leads to a specific physical act (playing their best to win the game). Even if the pep talk works well and the people are able to play at 100% morale, the players are unlikely to remember specific pep talks years later—or even minutes after they've happened.

When Inspiration strikes, there is no specific goal in mind. Inspiration may come from any source and at any time. The underlying Desire that is present combines with that Inspiration to create the "perfect storm" that moves you toward your desired goal. Inspiration is not specific to the outcome, but rather a force that each individual applies on their own to move forward toward achieving Success.

When I was overweight, I had the Desire to lose the weight. There were times when I would feel *motivated* to lose weight. For instance, when my Doctor told me that I had high blood pressure, I got a little scared; I was, at the time, motivated. When my doctor told me what might happen to me if I didn't make any changes, the imagery in my head was, however long it stayed, motivating. My *physical* reaction to that motivation was to exercise and eat better, but since that motivation was fleeting, I was often right back where I had started—and usually even heavier each time.

This changed when I reconnected with Anita. After that, I was more than motivated; I was Inspired. I knew that if she could change her life through diet and exercise, then I could as well. Her story served as my Inspiration which, combined with my Desire, created my "perfect storm." The Inspiration I got from Anita wasn't fleeting. When I combined it with the other Building Blocks of Success, I achieved my goal.

Different Stages of Inspiration

Inspiration isn't a fleeting force, but that doesn't mean that your source of Inspiration will always stay the same. As you progress on your journey, you may find Inspiration from other people or sources. That additional Inspiration will help you continue forward toward achieving your dream.

My friend Anita was my Inspiration for starting my health and fitness journey, and she continues to inspire me—but as I progressed on my journey I also found Inspiration from others, and those people helped to fuel me. Anita had achieved an amazing result, but she had done so by eating healthy and exercising moderately. As I got deeper and deeper into my Ironman training, I realized that I needed some additional Inspiration to help keep me going; as my goals changed over time, so did the type of Inspiration that I needed.

I started following triathletes on Facebook. I began reading magazines dedicated to the sport of triathlon. And then, one day, I saw a video on YouTube about a man named Ben Davis.

The video was the story of a young man who was severely obese. He struggled with relationships, self-esteem, and many of the same issues that I'd struggled with as an obese person. Ben decided to change his life and he did. He started with nutritional changes, like I did, and then moved into physical activity. He became a runner, then a triathlete, then eventually became an Ironman after losing 120 pounds. His story resonated with me because it was almost identical to mine. Like with my friend Anita, I realized that if he could do it, I could too. During my Ironman training, even when things were going well, I would often watch Ben's videos. After Anita, Ben became a source of Inspiration to me as well.

When Inspiration Fades

While the people or things that inspire you may change over time, there may be times when you feel like your Inspiration is fading. It happened to me in 2012 after I was forced to withdraw from Ironman Louisville. That is a day that I will never forget.

"Hey, baby," I said quietly.

"Hey," she said back with hesitation. "You okay?" she asked softly. I could hear the concern in her voice.

"I'm all right. I just don't think I can go on. I think I'm done. It's over." Part of me couldn't believe that I was actually saying those words aloud.

With a few little words, my Dream of becoming an Ironman had crumbled. At the time it seemed like the hardest conversation I'd ever had, and beyond it I felt like my world was falling apart.

For the months leading up to Ironman Louisville, all I could think about was how I couldn't wait to hear my name called out to the crowd and the finish line announcer yelling out that famous tagline: *Mark Rucker, you are an Ironman!* But as I sat there in the grass, on the side of Old Ballard School Road, I could only think about the crushing weight of disappointment on my shoulders. I thought about all of the time and effort that I invested in my training, all of the money that I spent for the race and equipment and supplies. I thought of all of the people who had come to cheer me on. At that moment, it was more than I knew how to bear. For a few moments, sitting defeated on the side of the road, I broke down and wept.

It was one of the lowest points of my life.

I started to play back my day up to that moment. Everything had started off *great*. I stayed in Lexington the night before the Ironman so I could get a good night's sleep in my own bed. I had my usual breakfast which provided me with a sense of comfort and familiarity. I packed up the last items and I headed out with my wife for Louisville. Once I got to the race check-in, I checked my bike, put my water and Gatorade bottles in my bike cages, and pumped up my tires. Then I went to body marking and got in line for the swim start.

The swim, which was 2.4 miles, went as planned. At the time, I had only been swimming regularly for about five months, so I was a very slow swimmer. I anticipated being in the water for about 2 hours. I came out after 2 hours and 14 minutes, but without any of the cramping I'd had a month earlier at Ironman Muncie. I felt *good*; I was off to a good start! I was out of the river and was ready for my favorite leg of the Ironman: the bike ride, all 112 miles of it.

I made it through the swim-to-bike transition in good time and mounted the bike to hit the road. I had ridden the course four separate times during previous practice sessions, and I knew that I could handle all the hills. But as I made my way away from the water and down River Road, I realized that something was wrong. My anticipated 18-19 mph pace on the bike was down to 13-14 mph. I figured it was residual from the swim; maybe I was just having trouble "finding my legs" after the swim. I convinced myself that I'd come around, so I kept pedaling.

When I made it to the first big hill, my average pace dropped to around 6 mph. I knew something wasn't right but I kept pushing. I felt my heart rate spike; I started feeling light-headed; I got a punishing headache, and I eventually threw up a few times— but I kept going.

Finally, at Mile 21, I got off my bike. I decided to check it just to see if there was a mechanical problem, and upon closer inspection I realized that I had made a *big* mistake. See, each athlete in Ironman is assigned a race number; that number is printed on multiple stickers that you're required to stick on your helmet and bike. I realized that, when I'd put my sticker on my bike frame, I had inadvertently wrapped my rear brake cable up with it—meaning that, for 21 miles, I'd been riding with my rear brake on. When I realized what I'd done, I was angry at myself for not checking the bike more carefully out of the water. Still, I was happy to figure out that it was a mistake I could fix, and I did. Like a flash I was back on the bike and back in the race.

Just like new, the bike moved like I thought it should. But as I looked at my time and average pace, I realized that I had to push harder to make up for the time I had lost. As I pushed myself harder, I started feeling sick again. It was a continual back-and-forth of resting briefly to recover, then pushing hard again to the point of sickness.

The bike route for Ironman Louisville includes a giant 32-mile loop that, in the course of the 112 miles, you end up completing twice. The loop takes you through downtown LaGrange, Kentucky, and LaGrange has a big festival during the Ironman where there are thousands of people in this tiny little town in the middle of nowhere cheering and screaming for all of the cyclists. As I got into LaGrange, the roar of the crowd energized me. I saw my wife and friends cheering for me. I quickly forgot about the sick feeling I had been fighting for the past hour and focused on pushing myself with renewed vigor.

And then, almost as quickly as the energy had hit me, it burned off. Soon I was outside of LaGrange on a small, one-lane country road surrounded by rolling hills. The crowds were all gone; there weren't many other cyclists around. My mind started to play tricks on me. The voice inside my head became louder and louder, telling me that I couldn't do this. *I'll never be an Ironman. I don't deserve to be an Ironman.* I got sick again. Around Mile 48, I made the decision to pull off the road.

As I sat in the grass, reflecting on the day, having my meltdown, a bike tech on a motorcycle stopped to check on me. She loaned me her phone so I could call my wife. She also called the SAG (support and gear) truck and told them to come and pick me up. She sat there with me for a few minutes even though she didn't have to; she seemed like she wanted to. As much as I wasn't in the mood for company at that moment, I'm glad she stopped for me.

She told me that pushing myself beyond the limits wasn't going to prove anything. She talked to me about all of the other Ironman events she had worked in the past, and she told me that, at all but one, at least one competitor had died. That really hit home with me. This is a *race*, invented on a whim by some of the best athletes in the world; it wasn't meant to be where people died. I had the chance to share my story with her as we sat there. She went on and on about how incredible my journey had been, how proud my family and friends must be.

She told me something that made me laugh. She said, "It's not the destination that matters, it's the journey."

She was right.

But it still bothered me when, for several months after the race, I struggled to stay focused on my goal. I slipped back into some old eating habits I'd been proud to lose. I didn't exercise regularly anymore. My running and swimming had stopped almost completely. Even cycling, my favorite of the three triathlon sports, was sporadic at best; the bike picked up dust sometimes.

I honestly felt like I had lost my Inspiration for good. Then—as it always does—something else happened.

Earlier in the year, I had won a trip to Hawaii to watch the Ironman World Championship in Kona. The trip was the grand prize offered by the headphone company Yurbuds as part of its "Beyond the Wall" competition. The contest involved posting a picture of yourself showing how you went "Beyond the Wall" and the winner was chosen by voters on the Internet. I finished in second place in the voting, but the company was so impressed with my story that they decided to award me with the Grand Prize as well.

So in October 2012, my wife and I were flown to Hawaii, all expenses paid, to see the Ironman World Championship. It was the best thing that could ever have happened to me. I got to see the top athletes in the world compete at the biggest event in the triathlon world. I even had the chance to meet one of the oldest Ironman competitors, Lew Hollander, who was competing that year at the age of 82. Talk about an Inspiration!

I returned home with a renewed sense of excitement. I had rediscovered my Inspiration. I could feel it from deep down again; I knew that I had no other option than to pick myself up, get back on the plan, and finish what I had started.

Being a Source of Inspiration for Others

A funny thing can happen sometimes when you start your own journey. As you share with others about your Dream and the actions that you are taking to achieve that Dream, you will *become* an Inspiration for others. That, in turn, can help serve as an Inspiration back to you.

When I started my journey, I decided to post about it on social media. For me, it was a way to keep myself accountable and to also, hopefully, inspire other people. Over time, as I lost weight and started completing my races, I had people reach out to me to tell me that I inspired them.

Excuse me, *what?*

I couldn't believe it. A guy who had been so obese, so out of shape—he was actually inspiring others now? I was in shock, but I loved it. And it was part of my Dream.

After I wasn't able to finish Ironman Louisville in 2012, I was worried about how people would respond to me. Would they think of me as a failure? Would people stop connecting with my journey? I really wasn't sure what the reaction would be.

Once I decided to resume my training in October 2012, I had a lot of people reach out to me to tell me that they had been following my story and were waiting to see how I'd respond to the setback I faced in Louisville. They all said the same thing: my decision not to give up had inspired them. I knew then that I had made the right decision.

Still, today, two years after becoming an Ironman, I still have people who tell me that I'm an Inspiration to them. The feeling that I get from that never changes; it's extremely humbling. But it also makes me very thankful, and happy.

You can have that same effect on people when you pursue your dreams. You can be an Inspiration to others. It is truly an amazing feeling—especially when you never expected to have it.

We have now discussed the Dream Stage of Success and the two Building Blocks of Success that comprise that Stage: Desire and Inspiration. Now we transition into the second Stage of Success: the Planning Stage.

CHAPTER THREE
VISION

"Where there is no vision, the people perish."
— *Proverbs 29:18 (KJV)* —

This Proverb was written by King Solomon to the people of Israel. It is one of the better-known of the Proverbs and is one of my personal favorites. Solomon was one of the wisest men ever to live, and his Proverbs were a guide for the people of Israel in their day-to-day lives.

This particular Proverb addresses what happens when a person, or people, lose their vision: they lose their way. As the Proverb related to the Israelites, it meant that when the people ignored God's Word, they would lose their way to sin and would be separated from God eternally.

In an application of this Proverb to your journey it means that even if you have a Desire and you have Inspiration, if you fail to have a Vision, then you cannot be successful in accomplishing your Dream. You will fail, plain and simple.

Your Vision is your road map. It is your plan. Just as a ship's captain must plan its course, so too must we plan our journey as we seek to achieve our Dream. It's not always easy, and sometimes that Vision may change, but it's imperative to have a Vision to be successful in your endeavor.

What Is Vision?

One of my favorite movies as a teenager was *Vision Quest*. It was the story of a high school wrestler, played by Matthew Modine, who wanted to become the state wrestling champion. The twist was that he wanted to become the champion at a lower weight class than the weight class in which he wrestled. He wanted to do this because the current state champion—in the lower weight class, below his—had never been defeated throughout his entire career. Modine simply wanted a shot to take down the best wrestler in the state. The movie focuses on the ups and down he faces as he struggles to accomplish his dream. In the end, he achieves his Dream and gets the girl (of course).

The movie derives its title from the Indian ritual called the "Vision Quest" which traditionally marked the rite of passage of a teenage boy into manhood. The young Indian male would typically go out into the wilderness on his own, for several days and nights, in search of his spiritual guide that would direct him on his path in life. It was a defining moment in a young boy's life, as the quest would usually cast a vision for what his life would become.

Of course, real life isn't always like the movies, but casting a vision for the Dream you want to achieve is essential for success. And for this reason, Vision is the 3rd Building Block of Success.

Stop for just a moment. Grab a sheet of paper and a pen. Now take just a moment and think about what it is in life that you want to accomplish. What is your Dream? You are reading this book for a reason—probably to help you to achieve success in some area of your life. Now take a moment and just write down your Dream. It doesn't have to be a full page or even a paragraph. It might be one sentence or even just a few words. But write down your Dream now.

OK. Are you done? Now read those words to yourself. Read it out loud. Commit it to memory. Done?

Now ball up the piece of paper and throw it away.

What? I go to the effort to write down my Dream and then you want me to throw it away? Why would I do that? Work with me on this for a moment.

In the past, when I would set a Vision for myself, I always focused on my "end goal." If it was health and fitness, then my end goal would sound something like "lose 100 pounds." Then, I would set off on my journey to lose 100 pounds.

Usually I would be successful for 3 or 4 weeks; I would start eating healthy, I would start exercising, and I would go at it 110%. The problem was that I would spend so much time focusing on my end goal that I would lose sight of the *small* successes I was experiencing already. I would get so stuck on the fact that I had 90 pounds to go and ignore that I'd done well so far by losing 10 and getting started. Eventually, I would get so frustrated that I would simply give up.

Are you like that? I think most of us are. We set an end goal and we become so blind by focusing on that end goal; we lose sight of all of the good we can do, and experience, along the way. When we don't reach the end goal in a set amount of time—usually as fast as we *want* something—we give up. I did that over and over and over again in my adult life when it came to my health and weight.

When I started this journey in February 2011, I took a different approach from anything I had ever tried before. It worked for me, and I know it will work for you.

You're not still holding onto that piece of paper, are you? Trust me on this. Throw it away.

The Value of Small Steps

When I started my journey in 2011, my Desire was to lose weight and get healthy. After my experience on my family vacation in Tennessee, it was my priority to regain my health, become active, and be a participant in my life and the lives of my family members. At almost 400 pounds, that was becoming impossible to do. Just being healthy would have been a major improvement.

Even so, there was another part of me that, more than being healthy, wanted to be an Ironman. It was an idea that truly fascinated me. I think it started it law school; I was very overweight when I started law school, and during my last two years I made an effort to try to get active, so I started running and cycling and lost weight (though I wasn't able to keep it off). As I started running and cycling, I started imagining what it would be like to compete in one of those epic races. I had seen footage of the World Championship in Kona on TV and was in awe of what those athletes were able to accomplish. As my level of physical activity declined and my weight increased after law school, the thought of ever becoming an Ironman faded away—until I started my journey back to health in 2011.

When I had my "aha" moment in February 2011, I realized that I was not then in good enough physical condition to engage in much physical activity. I decided that I really needed to focus on my diet, to start with what I could change to help make my body healthier. I started with my biggest weakness: soft drinks. I was really addicted to Coke; I would drink the equivalent of a 2-liter of regular Coke (or more) each day. As a daily habit, it obviously added a tremendous helping of calories to my daily intake.

I decided that, instead of going cold turkey, I would switch to diet soda and then slowly cut it out altogether. I bought a 24-pack of Coke Zero that I kept at the office. Each day, I would allow myself to have one 12-ounce can. I made the decision that, once the 24-pack was gone, I would be finished with soda. Each day, I focused on drinking more water. Over the 24 days, I found that my craving for soda diminished and I actually started craving water. After the last Coke Zero was gone, I stuck to my commitment and quit drinking soda.

I also knew this much from past "diets": I couldn't quit everything all at once. Although that method of change had yielded successful results in the past, they were *always* short-lived results. Any weight loss would be immediately restored out once I would self-destruct and revert back to my old habits. This time I knew that it wasn't just going to be a "diet" so much as a whole lifestyle change.

The next step was to cut out processed carbs. That was the single focus of the second week on my journey. I knew that breads, rice, and pasta were easy ways to add calories that I really didn't need in my diet. I focused on adding fruits and vegetables to my diet in an effort to replace the processed carbs with whole carbs. Instead of eating bread for lunch, I would pack a salad loaded with tons of different veggies. Instead of having cereal in the morning, I would eat an egg substitute omelet with sautéed veggies and a side of fruit.

Within these first two weeks, I could already feel a difference in my body, and I could see it too. I felt healthier; I had more energy. I had lost weight, so my clothes fit better. I honestly started to believe that I could do this, that I *could* change my life by taking small steps.

Each week, I would focus on making another small change to my eating habits. The week after I cut out the processed carbs, I decided to focus on my snacks. I am a huge fan of almonds, but for years I had been eating them roasted and salted, thinking that I was doing myself a favor. Unfortunately, the roasting removes a lot of the nutrients, and all the salt isn't healthy for someone who had high blood pressure at the time. So I decided to eat raw almonds each day instead. I remember the first time I bit into one; I thought it was spoiled. It was slightly sweet and chewy. The almonds I'd always eaten were salty and very crunchy. I threw the pack away and bought another. Again, I had the same sweet, chewy experience. Then it hit me: the almonds that I had grown accustomed to were crunchy because all the moisture (and sweetness) had been roasted out of them. I honestly felt a little stupid when I realized that *this* was how an almond was really supposed to taste. Now I love the taste of raw almonds.

The next step for me was to cut out salad dressing. I love Ranch dressing. Let me say that again, and louder: **I LOVE RANCH DRESSING.** Good Lord, I think if you covered an old leather boot with enough Hidden Valley, I could probably figure out a way to eat it. But that's also proof it's bad for you, and even back then I knew that dressing added a lot of needless calories to my diet. Sure, I know there are fat-free dressings and I'm not saying they're terrible for you, but I wanted to do as much as I could, and for me that meant cutting out all the items in my diet that I could live without. I would add a little olive oil to my salad instead of dressing, just for the mild flavor and texture, but eventually I even stopped adding olive oil to cut out the fat calories. It took some time to get used to eating raw veggies in a bowl, but now I love it. I am *still* amazed at how my tastebuds got used to food always being covered in dressings, salt, and sugar. Now I love the taste of raw fruits and veggies by themselves.

The next step was to cut out alcohol. Words like that, I know, are blasphemous in Kentucky Bourbon country, but by this point I was able to look at it from a simple calorie-intake perspective. Food and drink are to be enjoyed—but when the calories added by those items outweigh their return for you, it's time to make a change. It was tough to go out with friends and not drink, but I did what I knew and felt I had to.

Now you know the dietary changes that I made on my journey, and you can see, through that example, that everything I did was broken into small steps. Changing one small thing each week led to huge changes over time.

Just so you know, it would be wrong to say that I *never* eat processed carbs now. I drink beer or wine sometimes, even a soft drink every now and again, but they aren't regular staples in my diet these days like they once were. For my journey to be successful, I knew that I had to prove to myself that I could reach a point where I could exercise self-control over the things that helped get me so out of shape. Now I know that I have the ability to exercise that self-control.

After implementing the small-steps philosophy in my nutritional regimen, and having a lot of success with it, I decided it was time to apply it to my exercise routine (or lack thereof).

I didn't get off to the greatest of starts. The first entry in my training journal, from my first day back to physical activity, just reads: "That was awful!" That's about all I can say about my first bike ride in 15 years; I rode a total of around 3 miles at about a 9 mph pace (which, for a bike ride, is a very short distance at a very slow speed). I was so frustrated afterwards that I decided that I was going to put my bike up and not ride again. When I put it away, it stayed away for a couple of months.

After that terrible beginning, I decided to start walking on my lunch break at work. I started with just one mile. I remember feeling dead tired after each walk. And I was *sooooooooooooo slooooooooooooow*. Sometimes it would take me as long as 20 minutes to walk a mile. But I stuck with it. After a couple of weeks, I walked more than just one mile. I started getting faster.

After walking for a month or so, I was able to walk 3-4 miles each day and hitting a pace of about 16 minutes per mile. So, then, I decided that I wanted to try running.

I did some research and found a program called Couch 2 5K. I was then a member of an online fitness community called DailyMile.com and I had seen several people talking about the program. I also found an app from Bluefin Software called Couch 2 5K (now called Ease Into 5K, last I checked). I decided to give it a try. The journal entry from the first day of that reads:

> First day of the Couch to 5K program.
> That wasn't fun either.
> But at least I did the whole workout.

That was April 18, 2011. I decided to go to a local park after work to start the program for myself. I was wearing brand-new shoes and my iPhone app was all ready to go. The program is set up in intervals, so you begin with a 5-minute warm-up walk. Then, the program alternates between periods of running and walking for 20 minutes. You finish with a 5-minute cool-down walk. I remember feeling embarrassed and thinking that everyone was looking at me. I convinced myself that they were all saying to themselves *why is that fat guy trying to run?* Again, mentally I was frustrated—but I stuck to the program.

I continued with Couch 2 5K and ran my first full 5K on July 4, 2011. I felt *amazing*. This time, the entry read:

> That was so much fun!
> Finished my first 5K in 17 years.
> The Great Buffalo Chase is in the books!

I was pretty proud of myself, but I didn't waste any time. I immediately went into training for my first 10K. I found another app from Bluefin Software called Bridge 2 10K (for some reason all of these exercise apps *must* use the numeral 2 in place of the two-letter word). It was the same type of program as Couch 2 5K. It started with a warm up, followed by intervals of running and walking (all of which are prompted by the app saying "walk" or "run"), followed by a cool-down walk. Using that app, I was able to successfully complete my first 10K on July 30, 2011, only 26 days after running my first 5K in years.

At that point, I decided to keep going. It really became more of a challenge for me, just to see how far I could go—and, quietly, those old thoughts of Ironman started creeping back into my head. I told my friends that I would keep pushing myself until my body told me to stop. I continued to walk at work on my lunch breaks, to run three times a week for training, and then I started riding my bike again.

I found another app by Bluefin called Hal Higdon's Half Marathon Training Plan. Hal Higdon is a well-known running coach and I decided that the program would be a good fit for me because I could use my iPhone to track everything. This app was different, though, in that there were no more intervals. The runs were in miles, not minutes. There was no walking in the middle anymore. Even with the differences from what I was used to, I was able to follow the program, and I finished my first half-marathon, the Iron Horse, in Midway, Kentucky, on October 23, 2011.

That still wasn't enough for me. I kept going. Fortunately, Bluefin had developed another app during the time that I was training for my half marathon called (you guessed it) Hal Higdon's Marathon Training Plan. It was just like the half marathon plan (except not half) and I followed it the same way; the only difference was that this plan added a fourth day of running in the middle of the week. This was probably the toughest part for me because I was training outside during the winter, so I was running in some pretty miserable conditions. You might be surprised, though, at how nice the nice moments could be in that cold. I definitely had some amazing moments, like January 15th when I ran 21 miles for the first time. My training journal entry for that day simply reads:

> 21-mile solo run. Awesome!! That is all.

Just a month later, exactly 10 months to the day that I started Couch 2 5K, I ran and completed my first marathon in Myrtle Beach. Imagine how I felt then.

> Woot woot!! I'm a marathoner!! Slower than I had hoped but what an AMAZING day! I can't even put into words what this experience means to me.
>
> Thank you all SO much for all of your support and encouragement along this incredible journey.

I think that journal entry sums it up.

After the marathon, my training attention turned straight to the Ironman. I was running and cycling but I needed to add swimming. I had taken swim lessons when I was about 6 years old at the local YMCA, and I think I made it to the level of "Pollywog," but that was the extent of my swimming. So I joined a local gym and started my swim training on my own.

I really didn't have a plan for my swimming. There was no app. No coach. Just me and the pool at 5:00 am. Each week in the pool I just kept trying to push myself to go farther. I wasn't focused on speed. I just needed to get the distance.

And it wasn't easy.

> That was terrible. I am not a good swimmer. At all.

That was a training journal entry from April 2012. Swimming was tough. But just like the walking and the running I stuck to it. And I also started focusing on my cycling as well.

As of the beginning of May 2012, the farthest I'd ever ridden was 28 miles. I knew that by July 7, 2012 I'd have to be up to 56 miles for Ironman Muncie and by August 26, 2012 I'd have to be up to 112 for Ironman Louisville. So I continued to push myself and on May 12th I did a practice ride on the Ironman course in Louisville. I was very excited about that ride as my journal entry shows:

> Just rode 66 miles on the Ironman Kentucky bike route in Louisville. My longest ride ever up to this point had been 28 miles. That's a new distance PR by 38 miles! Ha!
>
> What the mind believes the body can achieve I guess, huh? Hope you guys are having an awesome Saturday! I'm sore as hell but I can't quit smiling.

Then, just two weeks later, I rode my first century ride (100 miles) when I completed the Horsey Hundred in Central Kentucky with the Bluegrass Cycling Club.

From there, I just continued to train in all three sports and on July 7, 2012, I completed my first triathlon ever, the half-Ironman in Muncie, Indiana.

Just two days later, I was back in the pool continuing to push myself toward the goal of achieving the full Ironman swimming distance of 2.4 miles. And as you can see from my training journal entry, I was able to hit my goal:

> Awesome swim. A new distance PR of 4000 meters and that gets me to the full Ironman distance of 2.4 miles too. What a great way to kick off my week.

As I mentioned earlier, I wasn't successful in my Ironman attempt in 2012, but I didn't let it stop me, and I went back in 2013 and finished what I had started. By the end, I was 130 pounds lighter than I was when I had started my journey back in 2011.

I know that not all of you reading this have the desire to be an Ironman. Plenty of people have told me I'm crazy for having that passion. But since you *are* reading this book, you have the Desire to make a change in some aspect of your life. And hopefully you have found your Inspiration as well. Now you need to develop your Vision. And that is where the small-steps philosophy is essential. It may take time to reach your ultimate Dream, but by taking small steps you can reach any goal that you set.

Will My Vision Change Over Time?

When I started my journey, my goal was to be healthy. I didn't set out to "lose 130 pounds." I didn't set out to be an Ironman—but my Vision shifted as my journey unfolded. As I took small steps towards being healthy, I was able to refine my Vision and focus on becoming an Ironman.

Earlier in the chapter, I asked you to write down your dream, then I told you to wad it up and throw it away. The point is this: it's important to know what your end goal is, but your end goal is likely to change over time, and you have to change with it. When the goal does shift, you don't want to be stuck chasing an *idea* of what you want that, in reality, you've long since balled up and thrown away.

Weight loss (and overall health) was my end goal—at first. But as I continued my journey, I was able to refine that Dream into the Ironman Dream. You may find that your Vision will need to adapt over time as well.

Perhaps you want to find financial success—maybe that is your end goal. As you start taking your small steps toward achieving that Dream, you may find that you refine that goal into a more specific goal. Maybe you'll realize that a promotion at work, for instance, is the step that will help you accomplish your financial success. In turn, you will need to lay out the small steps that you can take to make that promotion happen.

These things change over time. Be flexible.

The Value of Sharing Your Vision

I wrote about my dear friend Anita in Chapter 2, how she inspired me to begin my journey in 2011. Anita's doctor gave her some pretty straightforward marching orders: he wrote four short instructions on a sheet of paper for her to follow, and they worked. The last of his instructions? *Tell no one that you are trying to lose weight.*

Wait, what?

I know that seems counterintuitive. At least, it does to me. Over the years, when I was trying a new diet plan or exercise routine, I wanted *everyone* to know about it. I'd usually share how hard it was and, with the right people, how miserable I was. Are you like that? I think many of us are.

But Anita's doctor told her that, many times, when we tell others about our efforts to lose weight, they become unintentional saboteurs. Think about it. How many times, when you're around people and food and you mention that you can't have something, does someone then say, "Oh, just one little piece won't hurt you"? They aren't trying to be the devil on your shoulder or sabotage your diet; most of the time, they're just trying to be nice. But if people *don't* know that you're on a diet, and you simply don't draw attention to the fact that you're declining something unhealthy, usually no one says anything. It's only when people know that you're trying to eat better that they (unintentionally) sabotage you.

For Anita, that plan worked. She dropped off social media for quite some time while she was focused on losing weight. When she finally reappeared on Facebook, she had lost 180 pounds. I'd say her plan worked and then some.

But it's different in my case. I'm a bit of a social media addict, and I share quite a bit on Twitter and Facebook. I decided from Day One that I was going to share this journey with everyone. I shared the good and I shared the bad; I shared the successes and I shared the failures. I even shared a few pictures of the black toenails and bloody nipples that I sustained from the long-distance running (and yes, those lost me a few followers).

My reasons were, to me, simple. I wanted to share my experience with others in the hope of inspiring them to start their own journeys. If someone could see me struggling every day to change my life and they were inspired by that, my struggle would become that much more meaningful to me. My second reason for sharing was simply to provide me with some accountability.

In the first six months of my journey, I did everything by myself. I walked alone. I ran alone. I cycled alone. I was too embarrassed to work out around other people because of my weight. Still, I posted all of my workouts on social media. I used a great app called Cyclemeter that would track my workouts and post to Twitter and Facebook every time I started a workout. My social media friends could see that I was walking or running, and if they commented, the app would read the comments to me. So, while I was technically alone, I connected in a way that allowed me to hear my friends cheering me on as I exercised. It was such an important part of my early journey.

The cheering was important, and a great boost, but the more important part of it was the accountability it allowed me to create for myself. If I wanted to skip a workout, I could post about it—and my friends would encourage me not to skip it. If I missed a few days, my friends would check on me to see what was going on and why I breaking my workout pattern.

As I became more focused on my running and started running with a group, I shared my Vision with those other runners. I told them that I wanted to run a half-marathon; later, I told them that I wanted to run a marathon. Both times, they supported me and encouraged me. They helped me reach those milestones. Then, when I moved on to triathlon training, I worked out with other triathletes and shared my Vision of being an Ironman with them, and once again they helped me achieve that Dream.

Vision is very personal. If you are the type who prefers to work alone and you don't like sharing personal things with others, then by all means, keep your

Vision to yourself. You're not doomed for failure simply because you're not the sort to share with others. But if you're like me, and you *are* very social, and you do like to share with others, then I would encourage you to talk openly about what you see and want. Talk about your Vision with others. In my case, talking about it allowed me to develop a deep network of support and accountability, and it connected me in a way that allowed me to give back and inspire others along the way.

What if I Lose My Vision?

Earlier, we discussed how Vision can change over time and how you may need to refine it as you journey down your path of change. But what happens if you lose your Vision? What do you do when your original end goal no longer seems important?

In Chapter 1, we talked about the three stages of Desire and what can happen during those stages. If you find that your Vision has not simply changed over time, but has altogether vanished, then it may be more of a matter of your Desire, since your Vision will be a natural extension of your Desire. And if you find that you no longer seem to know which direction to go, then your Desire may be waning.

Before you simply give up on your Dream, I would encourage you to spend some time away from things. A short break may give you the clarity that you need to refocus and regain your Vision. I took a break after my failed Ironman attempt in 2012; not only did it help me to find my Desire again, but it also helped me redefine the steps that I needed to take to realize that Dream.

I would also recommend that you spend some time talking with others about your loss of Vision. Sometimes a fresh perspective can be all that we need to help us realize where we can make some changes, and those changes can get us back on track to achieving our Dreams.

This brings us to the fourth Building Block of Success: Knowledge.

CHAPTER FOUR
KNOWLEDGE

*"To know what you know and what you do not know,
that is true knowledge."*
— *Confucius* —

Many people think of *knowledge* as simply "how much they know" and never give deliberate thought to what they *don't* know. Confucius suggests that only when we acknowledge our ignorance, in addition to our knowledge, that we attain true knowledge. I've come to agree with him, although it took me quite some time to reach this conclusion for myself.

Knowledge of the higher sort requires that we allow ourselves to be vulnerable, but that, in so doing, we open ourselves to growth opportunities. That is why Knowledge is the 4th Building Block of Success.

What is Knowledge?

Knowledge is the "information, understanding, or skill that you get from experience or education." We can see from the last part that knowledge comes from two sources: (1) experience and (2) education.

Experience is relatively straightforward. As you undertake your journey, you will have experiences of your own that will increase your level of Knowledge about your Dream. You will learn what works for you and what doesn't work for you.

Experience is very individualized. What you learn from a particular event may not be the same as what someone else takes away from it. That's fine; your experiences are yours, and just as unique as your Dream.

Education, on the other hand, can be a little harder to define. Experience can provide an education of its own—most of us call that the "school of hard knocks." Of course, in this context, "education" is shorthand for formal education. For most of us, there is no formal educational setting for us to learn more about achieving our Dreams.

But what is there for us to educate ourselves?

Sources of Education

Is this modern day, many of us use the Internet to learn every day, though we don't always realize it. If I have question, like many people I Google the answer. If I have a question about how to do something, I will go to YouTube and search for videos showing me how to do it.

The same was true for my training. I really didn't know where to begin, so I searched the Internet for assistance and started reading. I discovered the "Ease Into 5K" app through my first Internet searches. After reading the reviews about it, I thought that it seemed appropriate and motivating to me—and sure enough, after using the nine-week program outlined in the app, I completed my first 5K. Later, I did more research on the Internet and found an app from the same company for 10K training, half-marathon training, and marathon training. I used them all and had a great deal of success with all of them.

Even as I moved into Ironman training, I used the Internet as a means for furthering my Knowledge. I frequented websites dedicated to beginner triathletes in an effort to learn more about the sport and about how to prepare myself. I was even able to find numerous free training plans online that I was able to download and use as I prepared for Ironman Louisville in 2012.

But, as you know, you do have to be careful with what you read on the Internet. Not everything you find is going to be beneficial to you; not everything you read will be true, or true for you. So if you use the Internet, do so with your eyes wide open. If you are going to purchase a program to assist you on your journey, make sure to read what others have to say about it. If, for example, your Dream were to achieve financial success, and you had found a program that claimed to offer you the key to riches, you would make sure that you had read the reviews first, lest you get sucked into someone else's scheme. Be smart, be careful, and if something sounds too good to be true, it probably is.

Another helpful source of Knowledge is books. Yes, I said it. Just like high school or college, you do have to "hit the books" sometimes. When I began my journey, I invested in a few books about running; likewise, as I moved into triathlon training, I found a book called the *Triathlete's Training Bible*. This book was very helpful for me, as a beginner, in developing an understanding of the sport and of how to train in general.

I'm sure that, whatever your Dream may be, you will be able to find a few books to help you on your journey. Of course, I hope that you will consider this book to be one that is essential to your journey as a whole, but it is helpful to find books specifically related to your Dream. If you wanted to be the best husband you could be, I would suggest self-help books on developing relationships. If your Dream is to be the President of a company, I would suggest books on leadership and management—and so on. Whatever your dream, you will find books out there that will help you develop your Knowledge.

The same caveat applies: you need to be careful. As you look for books to assist you on your journey, don't fall under the impression that books are better if they're intense or super-detailed; if something intimidates or confuses you, it isn't helpful. I made this mistake with some of the running books that I bought and I ended up confusing myself more than helping.

It all goes back to the quote from Confucius. I didn't realize what I *didn't* know at the time and wasn't prepared to deal with all of it yet. This is why you should read reviews; see what others have to say. Is the book designed for someone who is just beginning or for someone with a solid grasp of the basics already? Make sure that you don't sabotage yourself by getting in over your head right away.

A third source of Knowledge is people. For me, this has been the biggest source of Knowledge. As a runner, I learned a lot from Internet research and from reading, but it wasn't until I began running as part of a group that I learned the majority of what I needed to know. When I had strange pains in my hip, I researched it online and came up with a variety of possible explanations, none of which seemed quite right. But when I asked my fellow runners what it could be, I instantly got the correct answer and learned how to deal with it at the same time.

This advice applies for any aspect of your life that you want to change. If you have an addiction problem that you want to overcome, attending meetings and being around others is a great source of Knowledge. When you surround yourself with those who have gained Knowledge through experience, then you can harness the power of *their* experience to enhance your own Knowledge.

The Value of Coaching

After my unsuccessful attempt at Ironman Louisville in 2012, I took some time away from training to figure out what I wanted to do. As I mentioned before, part of me wanted to quit training; the thought of going through all of the effort and time was a little overwhelming sometimes. But those moments of doubt were ultimately short-lived, and I knew that I needed to finish what I'd set out to achieve. It was my Dream, and I would not let it go without another fight.

As I began training for Ironman Louisville 2013, I knew that I needed to do something different. In 2012, I had done quite a bit of Internet research about triathlon training; I had read several books about it as well, and I had trained with a few people who had more experience than I did. But all of that wasn't enough to get me where I needed to be; I needed something more, and I knew it. My dedication was there and my Desire was there; I needed more Knowledge.

So I hired a coach.

In Lexington, we are fortunate to have several expert triathletes who not only compete, but who also coach others who want to learn more about the sport. I was fortunate to hire Beth Atnip, an experienced triathlete who had qualified and competed in the Ironman World Championship in Kona; Beth was also the Race Director for Ironman Louisville. Her knowledge of the sport, and of the race itself, was second to none.

I knew that having a coach would help me identify the areas where I had weaknesses; I knew that as a triathlete I had many, but I didn't know how to fix them. I acknowledged that having someone with the knowledge to identify those weaknesses would prove invaluable.

But it wasn't just the ability to identify my weaknesses that made we want to hire a coach. I knew that I would also benefit from the *motivation* provided by a coach. On the days where you just don't think you can finish your workout, your coach can give you the encouragement you need to stay focused and get the work done. Having a coach can provide a level of accountability that will help motivate you to keep moving forward.

There are coaches out there for almost every aspect of life: relationship coaches, financial coaches, life coaches, nutritional coaches, etc. You can find a coach for most kinds of self-improvement.

But how do you know if a coach is the right idea for you? And, if so, which coach is right for you?

For me, it was pretty easy to decide that I needed a coach. In my efforts to become an Ironman, I learned that I am the type of person who can get distracted when working on a big project. When I set my mind to achieve something, I almost always do it, but sometimes I take the long way. That long way can be time-consuming and extremely inefficient. I've always been something of a "check the box" person and I realized that I needed someone to provide some structure for my efforts—to give me tasks to complete so I could "check the box" as I completed my workouts.

As for picking a coach, that was pretty easy in my case. I already had a personal relationship with Beth since she was a member of the same triathlon club. She had given me advice in 2012 on my race preparation and I knew that she was a genuine, caring person who'd have my best interests at heart. But I also knew that, just as important, she was a successful triathlete who knew the sport. I also knew other people she was coaching and they all had great things to say about her.

With all of that information at hand, it was a no-brainer for me to hire her, and it paid off.

If you have reached a point in your journey where you feel like you have invested a lot of time in research and reading, and you've sought the advice and guidance of others to learn from their experiences but still need to gain more Knowledge, then I strongly suggest considering hiring a coach.

As with every other source of Knowledge that I've discussed so far, there are caveats for hiring a coach.

Make sure that the person you are thinking of hiring is someone you can get along with as a coach. Your prospective coach may be a great person, but if you don't have any chemistry with him or her, the coaching relationship may not work out and you may end up frustrated. Take some time to talk with your prospective coach to get to know her; coaches aren't free, and a prospective coach should anticipate that you want to be comfortable before you make that commitment.

You will also want to evaluate the experience of your prospective coach. How long has she been coaching? Is her area of expertise what you need? You don't want to hire a coach who has limited experience or knowledge in the specific area you need help in. Hiring a running coach would have been great for me as a runner, but would have done nothing for my swimming and cycling, which are equally important parts of a triathlon.

Finally, talk to others about your coach. Have they had success with her coaching? Is she easy to work with? Is she responsive? Again, you will be paying your coach money to help you out, so you deserve some answers to your questions. Don't feel bad for asking your prospective coach for references; again, she should anticipate that you are going to do your homework before making the investment.

How Long Should I Spend Developing My Knowledge?

As I've said before, your journey is unique to you. As you travel your path to success, you may find that the Knowledge you gain from searching the Internet is enough to get you where you need to be. You may find that spending time with others and harnessing the Knowledge of their experience is enough. There is no single answer to the question.

I spent almost a year and a half developing my Knowledge from information gathered from the Internet, books, and numerous other sources before I attempted Ironman Louisville in 2012. After my unsuccessful attempt, I spent another 10 months working with a coach to prepare myself for Ironman Louisville 2013. That period of time was enough to allow me to develop the Knowledge that I needed to be successful—but your journey may be completely different.

I will caution you at this point, though, to not spend too much time developing your Knowledge. That may sound strange, but there's something that you have to understand: *you will never know everything there is to know about a particular topic.* There will never be an end to the information you can find about it, and if you spend too much time developing your Knowledge, you may find that you never successfully transition to the next Building Block of Success. You will suffer "analysis paralysis."

I have been prone to this "disease" at various times in my life. I think we all are sometimes. It's good to be knowledgeable and prepared for things you want to do in life, but sometimes it's easy to fiddle away your time preparing rather than doing. We like to study all possible scenarios; we consider all possible outcomes. We try to gather as much information as we can to enhance our Knowledge. At certain points, though, it only means we're stalling. We fail to move forward for some reason, often that we are afraid: afraid of the unknown, afraid of failure, or even afraid of success. Whatever the reason, "analysis paralysis" can derail your Dream. So as you work to gain Knowledge about your Dream, remember that at some point you will need to take that first step. Otherwise, your Dream will never become your reality.

Another key point is not to stop your journey simply because you feel you don't know enough. This is a relative of analysis paralysis; the wheels are still spinning and the wish to move forward is there, but it just never happens.

When we completely stop the journey to success to gather more Knowledge, we hamstring our intentions of moving forward on our plans. This can be even more damaging to your success than analysis paralysis because putting the brakes on progress for lack of information is often an excuse; it's a reason we can give for stopping, and we may never have to start again. If you find that you reach this point, what you may really need is to spend some time re-evaluating your level of Desire.

Knowledge is essential to success, but don't overthink your efforts to enhance that Knowledge; you only need to know enough to achieve your end goal.

Is It Ever Too Late to Seek Knowledge?

They say knowledge is power. I believe that it's never too late to learn more.

I spent 18 months training to become a runner, a swimmer, and a cyclist. I researched. I read. I spent time talking to other runners and swimmers and cyclists to gain their valuable Knowledge. Even after all that time, I still didn't have enough Knowledge about the sport of triathlon to get me where I needed to be to be successful.

While many people might have given up after an unsuccessful attempt, I chose not to, and when I went back I decided to improve my Knowledge in the sport further by hiring a coach. I spent an additional 10 months training with her, and that was exactly what I needed to achieve my Dream. Just because I had been unsuccessful the first time didn't mean that it was too late for me to learn what I needed.

I talk a lot about my Ironman training, but that's not the only area of my life where seeking out knowledge has proven beneficial. I also made the decision to hire a writing coach to help me learn what I needed to achieve my dream of becoming an author and a speaker.

In 2012, after my unsuccessful attempt at Ironman Louisville, I wanted to write a book about my health and weight loss journey. Even though my journey wasn't over then, and I still planned to achieve my Dream of becoming an Ironman, I knew that I wanted to share my story with as many people as I could to inspire them to change their lives, too.

In early 2013, while I was still training for Ironman Louisville 2013, my wife and I went to a local coffee shop and spent hours working on an outline for what I hoped would be my first book. I had read books about writing books, and I had researched it online, and one of the first steps seemed to be developing an outline. After completing the outline that day with my wife's help, I felt very positive about the project. I thought, then, that I would hammer out a book in no time.

Unfortunately, it didn't work out that way. Even though I had the Desire, the Inspiration, and the Vision to make it happen, I lacked the Knowledge. I didn't really know *how* to write a book.

My wife Annita, who is my biggest supporter and cheerleader, told me about a lady named Cathy Fyock whom she had met at a local conference a year or so before; Cathy was a speaker and an author, but she also worked as a coach to help aspiring writers learn about writing. My wife had encouraged me to reach out to Cathy but I never did. As time passed, my book went nowhere.

Finally, in mid-2015, I realized that the only way that I was going to make this Dream a reality was to seek assistance from someone like her, someone who had the Knowledge that I lacked. I reached out to Cathy and we decided to meet.

At our first meeting, Cathy went over the outline that I had written three years earlier and helped me develop it into (what is now) this book. She also helped me develop a routine for my writing that would keep me on track towards finishing the manuscript.

I realized that writing, for me, was similar to Ironman training. I could only go so far on my own; I needed additional Knowledge from someone else. I needed a coach, and once again it worked for me.

It's not the case that you have to hire a coach, trainer, or counselor for every Dream you want to accomplish. But it's important to realize your limitations when it comes to Knowledge and understand that seeking the help and guidance of someone who has that Knowledge can be exactly the right move.

Using Setbacks As a Source of Knowledge

As you travel your path to success, you will face setbacks along with the triumphs, tears along with the laughter. That's the way the journey to success is.

It's important to use the setbacks as learning experiences, then use that Knowledge to move yourself forward.

When Thomas Edison was asked about his numerous failures to create the incandescent light bulb, he replied that he hadn't failed, but rather, had found 10,000 ways that didn't work.

Can you imagine? Attempting something over and over hundreds and thousands of times and never getting it right? Most people would just give up. But if it's your Dream, then you don't give up. You keep moving forward—and you use the Knowledge you gain from your unsuccessful attempts to help propel yourself toward success.

I wrote before about the cycling portion of Ironman Louisville in 2012 and the fact that I wrapped my rear brake cable up with my athlete race number sticker. Honestly, it was one of the biggest rookie mistakes I could possibly have made. Still, as upset as I was at myself, and as disappointed as I was not to finish the race, I learned a very valuable lesson from that experience. I gained valuable knowledge that helped me the next year, when I went back and finished the race and became an Ironman. Trust me, all of my friends and family asked me before the race in 2013 if I had checked my wheels. *Lesson learned.*

CHAPTER FIVE
BELIEF

We have discussed the Dream stage of success—comprised of the two Building Blocks of Desire and Inspiration— and the Planning stage of success, which is comprised of the two Building Blocks of Vision and Knowledge. Now we conclude with the final Stage of Success, which is the Achieving stage. To begin the Achieving stage, let's discuss the fifth Building Block of Success: Belief.

What is Belief?

Webster's Dictionary defines *belief* as "a feeling of being sure that someone or something exists, or that something is true".

Think about that for just a moment. Let's break it down. First, it's a feeling of being *sure*. It's not merely feeling that something is a possibility, or thinking that something *might* happen. Belief is something much more. When you *believe* in something, you have moved beyond simply thinking it might happen. You are certain that it will happen.

Then there's the second part of that definition: "that someone or something exists, or that something it true." That is such a clean and reassuring thought: *that something is true*. When you have Belief, *you are sure that something is true*. Like all things do at first, it sounds simple, but it is one of the most difficult Building Blocks to master on your road to Success.

Why?

As we grow older, we wire ourselves to look at life with more cynical, more negative eyes. As a child, it's easy to dream and believe that we can do anything—but as we mature, and we suffer setbacks (or what we consider to be *failures*), it's easy to allow the voice inside of our heads to convince us that we *can't* do everything we wanted to do, that we can't achieve our Dreams, that we can't change our lives. That it's impossible to do what we want to do.

Belief in Yourself

When someone tells you that you need to "believe in yourself," how does it make you feel? It used to make me feel *bad*, almost like I wasn't doing something right. I couldn't figure out what they meant. Was I "doing life" wrong? Was there something that I was missing? When I "believed in myself," would I be believing in the wrong things?

I've come to realize though that the answer to those questions was *no*. I wasn't living wrong. I wasn't missing something. There wasn't something evading only me. But as I made my journey from a Couch Potato to an Ironman, I did realize *something* that I was doing wrong. I realized that I was wired to think in a negative way—and I think that many of us are wired that way.

As a young man, I seemed to be able to achieve anything that I wanted to achieve. In high school, I was pretty well-rounded; I was in band for several years and was first-chair baritone, but I decided as a junior that I wanted to quit the band and play football, so I did. I became a starting defensive tackle for my winning high school team. I also decided that I wanted to be on the academic team so I tried out and made it; it seemed that anything I wanted to do, I was able to do. Nothing seemed impossible.

I decided when I was 16 that I wanted to attend the University of Kentucky and become an attorney. I received a scholarship to UK and was very successful as a student there. I ran for student government and was elected; I interned for the Lieutenant Governor of Kentucky as a senior in undergraduate. I was a bartender at a popular local bar and a bass guitar player in a popular local band. I applied for only one law school, UK, and was accepted. Life became what I wanted it to be, or so it seemed.

I entered law school and decided to pursue my MBA at the same time; after four years, I earned both my MBA and JD.

And then the wheels came off.

I wanted to move to New York and become an attorney in Mergers and Acquisitions. I loved the movie *Wall Street* and the books by writers like Michael Lewis that told tales of the fortunes waiting to be made on Wall Street. I believed that, with my education and experience, I would be a shoe-in for a position with a big law firm—but when I graduated in 1994, we were in the middle of a recession. The boom of the late eighties on Wall Street was over, and the jobs just weren't there anymore. I sent out over 1200 resumes to firms in New York, Los Angeles, Chicago, Atlanta, Miami, and Boston and got zero responses. Not one. No one interviewed me.

I was crushed.

Add to all of this: I was married, we were expecting our first child, and I began to feel the pressures of life that I had never felt before. I had rent to pay, a wife to support, a child on the way, and thousands of dollars in student loans that were coming due very soon.

I shifted my goals and began looking for jobs locally with smaller firms, but I still had no luck. I spent the summer after I graduated from law school studying for the bar exam and trying to find work. (I ended up working at a local gym for minimum wage.) I passed the bar and was sworn in as an attorney in October 1994, but I still didn't have a job.

I began to struggle with depression and I chose to self-medicate with food and alcohol. I began to gain weight. As I gained more and more weight, my self-image began to deteriorate.

In November of 1994, I accepted a job as an attorney making $25,000 per year. That was about half of my total student debt at the time. I struggled to make ends meet with a wife and a new baby; life became increasingly difficult and I spiraled deeper into a pit of negative self-image. I wasn't the attorney I wanted to be; this was not the life I had envisioned for myself.

After six months at my job, I found another job making more money, but I was miserable at the new position. My boss was an extremely difficult person to work for, and after about a year, I left and started my own practice. I struggled at first, but was able to become successful on my own.

Unfortunately, the negative self-image hadn't left me. I still doubted my success and doubted my abilities as a father, as a husband, and as an attorney. I continued to struggle with depression and my eating and drinking worsened. Eventually, my wife and I divorced.

After my divorce, my negative thinking patterns started cutting deeper. I had failed as a husband and father. I didn't deserve to be happy; I didn't deserve to be successful. I was not a good person. These were thoughts that I struggled with daily, and they made life extremely difficult. My escape, as before, came through food and alcohol.

I remarried in 2000 to a wonderful woman, but the issues from my previous marriage prevented me from being the best husband that I could be. Or, I should say, I allowed my negative self-image to keep controlling my thinking patterns, and that affected every aspect of my marriage. My eating and drinking continued, and eventually I ballooned to 385 pounds.

I honestly didn't care about my health at that point. I thought that if I died as a result of my health issues, then it would just end my pain and unhappiness. It got to the point where I was so miserable with myself that my wife and I separated in 2004. How could someone who was so unhappy with himself ever bring joy to someone else? I believed that she deserved better.

Even though I had given up on myself, I'm thankful that my wife didn't give up on me. She encouraged me to go to church with her even though I told her that I didn't believe our marriage could be saved. The joke was on me: after going to church and counseling, we got back together and saved our marriage. I'm so thankful for her today, and she is truly my best friend and I can't imagine my life without her.

After we got back together, things seemed good for a while—but in 2007, the real estate market collapsed and my business fell apart. As a result, I had to close my doors after 11 years in business. Again, I felt like a failure.

I ended up taking a job in Missouri and my wife and I moved from Lexington. It was very hard on us; we missed my kids, and we both missed our families. We had an extremely difficult time adjusting to a new home, and I never really felt like I was accepted in my new position. I may have just been projecting my negative self-image, but nevertheless it was how I felt. And although our marriage was strong again, I still struggled with this overwhelming feeling that I was a failure and that I didn't deserve to be happy with my wife.

In 2010, we returned to Kentucky. I took a new job, and shortly thereafter, we took our family vacation to Gatlinburg, where I was too big to ride on the roller coaster with my daughter. That was when my Desire to change my life first took root. Even though it took another eight months for me to finally start making those changes, I did make them.

When I started my journey back to health, my thought process was overwhelmed with negative thoughts, like *you can't lose weight* or *you'll always be fat* or *you don't deserve to be happy*. There were times where I believed that little voice in my head and I wanted to give up, but still I didn't. I was able to overcome those negative thoughts every day by taking small steps towards my Dream.

The Flame of Greatness

A few years ago, Nike had a commercial featuring an overweight young boy running by himself on an empty road. The theme of the commercial was finding your greatness wherever you are in life. It's one of my favorite commercials; I've always remembered it.

That commercial is great because it really cements the idea of self-belief. We all have a flame of greatness inside of us. But for many of us, that flame has dwindled down over time to just a small and fluttering spark. Years of setbacks, failures, and self-doubt have created a pattern of negative thinking that has convinced us, quite wrongly, that our flame has burned out.

It hasn't. It's still there. It's burning. It just needs to be fed. You don't need to build a flame you don't have; you need to refuel the flame of greatness you already have.

But how?

It all goes back to the small-steps strategy that I discussed before. As you cast your Vision and you set small goals for yourself, you are developing the fuel for your fire. As you move forward and achieve those small goals, you fuel that flame of greatness. Each time you successfully complete a small step, you develop Belief in yourself and that becomes what feeds your flame of greatness. Eventually, your flame becomes a raging inferno that even you can no longer contain. Your flame burns hot and bright enough to become a light for others. It not only guides your path to success but is also lights the way for others to begin their own journey.

So how is *your* flame? Has it dwindled down to a small flicker over the years? I know that mine did. It's not failure to admit it—it's actually quite the opposite. It's an awakening. The first small step is realizing that things aren't the way you want them to be and then deciding that you want to change them.

Take those small steps. Feed that flame the fuel it needs. In what feels like no time by the end, your small flicker will develop into a raging inferno for the world to see. Not only will you regain that Belief in yourself, but you will become a beacon of hope to others as well.

Belief as Spirituality

When I speak of Belief in this book, I am speaking of Belief in self and the Belief in your Dream. But there is another level of Belief important to achieving any Dream, and that is the Belief in a Higher Power. I believe that my Belief in God has been a supporting source of all of my accomplishments.

Some of you may not believe in God, and that is your choice. I think for a while, during my darkest of days, I questioned whether God really existed because, if He did exist, I wondered how He could ever let me suffer as I did.

As I mentioned earlier, my wife and I separated in 2004. At the time, I wasn't happy with myself and I convinced myself that, if I couldn't be happy with myself, there was no way she could ever be happy with me. I believed that she deserved better; she deserved someone who could make her happy, and I wasn't that person.

I remember vividly the day that she asked me to go to church with her. I'd grown up in Eastern Kentucky in a Southern Baptist church. As a child, church was a weekly obligation; it was something I did because my parents made me go. At the time, I didn't think I got much out of it, but I know now that it laid a foundation for my character and the person I would eventually become. When she asked me to go, I looked her straight in the eyes and scoffed. "Sure, I'll go," I said, "but not even God can fix our marriage."

I was wrong.

Not only did attending church together provide us with the strength to heal our marriage, it also provided me with the faith that I never truly developed as a child. I read the Bible on a regular basis; I've even read the entire Bible from cover to cover in 90 days on two separate occasions. Each time, I spent the last 40 days of that time fasting. Yes, I fasted for 40 days; I drank only water and vegetable and fruit juices. No solid foods. Through those experiences, I developed a faith so deep that I knew that, whatever happened in my life, I would get through it.

Having faith doesn't mean that things always work out the way that I want them to, but my faith provides me with the knowledge that things will always work out as they are *supposed* to. That gives me hope through all the storms that I face in life.

So when I speak of Belief, I am referring to Belief in self and Belief in the Dream. But underlying that is a much deeper Belief that guides everything that I do in my life, and I hope you can find the equivalent for your own life.

Overcoming Self-Doubt

Developing Belief in yourself is essential to achieving your Dream and finding the success that you want for yourself. But how in the world do you overcome *years* of self-doubt? Do you just wake up one day and find it's magically gone away? Can you take a pill to make it disappear while you sleep? Is there a late-night infomercial where someone with an obnoxious voice and a bad haircut will sell me the kit for the low, low price of (just three easy payments of) $19.99?

No. It's not that easy. It takes a lot of hard work and discipline, and it takes constant effort to maintain. But it can be done.

I've talked about the small-steps strategy before, and I'd like to revisit it here. I cannot stress enough the importance of setting those small, incremental goals. They are essential to your Success. The more of those small goals you can achieve, the more that self-doubt will start to melt away, and the stronger your Belief in yourself will become.

When I first started running, I was embarrassed of how I looked (or at least how I thought I looked) that I stopped running at a nearby park because I didn't want anyone to see me. I found a fairly empty road close to my home that had very few houses along it, and that's where I ran, week after week. As my confidence grew in my running, I started running with friends. I actually ran races. I ran where people could see me! I didn't care what others thought. Sure, I was still a big guy. Sure, I was slow. But I was doing it! I was running, and no one could say or think or do anything to take that away from me. *I was a runner.* The longer the distances I ran, the more I believed in myself.

If you struggle with self-doubt like I did (do), you know that it can raise its ugly head at any time. So even after all I went through—losing 130 pounds, then running a 5K, a 10K, a half-marathon, a marathon, and a half-Ironman—I still doubted myself.

How could that be possible? you ask.

It's because of what happened at Ironman Louisville in 2012. After I made the decision to quit the race at Mile 48 on the bike ride, I felt like a complete failure. Everything that I had achieved up to that point went out the window. To me, none of it mattered. For a few months after that race, I found myself in a very dark place of self-doubt. I questioned why I'd been doing all of this. I even picked up some of old, bad eating habits again. I gained some weight.

But then I decided that I had to get back to the Dream, the Dream of being an Ironman. So I got back in the pool. I got back on my bike. I laced up my running shoes and hit the pavement again. It felt great when I did. Most importantly, I began to set small goals for myself again.

"Ride this far today," I'd tell myself.

"Swim 3500 yards today," I'd tell myself.

And I'd do it.

Over time, I was able to push those negative thoughts out of my head and replace them with the positive words of achievement.

I'll never forget the feeling of getting back on that bike again in Louisville in 2013. I had just swam 2.4 miles in an hour and half, cutting 45 minutes off my time from the year before. I felt great, but I was apprehensive.

What if I don't make it? I thought.

I got on the bike and pedaled anyway. I felt amazing. As I approached the point on the course where I'd given up the year before, I couldn't help but smile, and as a tear of joy rolled down my face I *knew* that I was going to do it. I *knew* that by the end of that day I would be an Ironman.

And so I was.

Others' Belief in You

I've written about the importance of surrounding yourself with positive people as you work to achieve your goals. Having a core group of like-minded people around you is essential to achieving the success that you desire. While the determination and dedication to reach your goals is yours alone, your Inspiration, Vision and Knowledge will all be impacted by other people. Having others who believe in you and your goals will carry you further than you can imagine.

After Ironman Louisville 2012, I was struggling to continue on my journey, and many times I felt like I might not be able to achieve my Dream. A big part of the problem was that some of the people I'd trusted and looked to for support turned their backs on me; at some point, I discovered that they had never believed I could complete the Ironman. They never shared their beliefs with me, but after the failed attempt in 2012 I found out that several of them took some degree of *schadenfreude* in my failure.

I was stunned. The people whom I'd trusted to lift me up and support me were secretly rooting against me. I suppose some of that is human nature; when someone else has success, it's difficult for others to like or accept it all the time. As I successfully completed race after race, perhaps my success was too much for them to accept, especially when they'd begun to believe certain challenges were over my head. They privately wished for me to fail, and after Ironman Louisville 2012 their attitude was *told you so*.

It took me months to come to terms with what I felt was betrayal by people I'd believed were my friends. Even today, it still hurts. Betrayal is one of the worst hurts that one person can inflict upon another, and forgiving doesn't necessarily mean forgetting.

Still, I was fortunate enough to have other friends who remained close and supportive during that difficult period. I remember being on a bike ride with two of these friends on a very chilly fall morning. I opened up and talked to them both about how I felt about not completing the race. I shared how I felt about the betrayal by people I thought were my friends. I even talked about just giving up because maybe those former friends had been right; maybe I couldn't do it.

My friends listened and supported me and offered me some amazing advice. They assured me that it was okay to feel the way I felt about everything. But they also told me something very important, something that I needed to hear. They told me that they believed in me.

It was as though a weight had been lifted off of my shoulders. The clouds dispersed. The sun, once again, had risen to shine on me and my Dream. *My friends still believed in me.* They believed that I could accomplish my Dream.

That small seed of Belief was all that I needed to get back in the game and to believe in myself again.

It is important, as you begin your journey, to surround yourself with positive people who will cheer your successes and help you nurse your wounds when you stumble and fall, friends who will stick with you regardless of the circumstances. Surround yourself with those with whom you can be open and honest. In return, extend the same to them. If you find that your friends question your Dream or seem to relish in your setbacks, they aren't true friends and you'd be better served to distance yourself from them.

Self-Belief vs. Arrogance

> *"My success isn't a result of arrogance. It's a result of belief."*
> — Conor McGregor, UFC Fighter —

Arrogance will never be a source of success for you, or for anyone. Success is the result of Belief—the Belief in yourself and your Dream.

With that being said, there can be a fine line sometimes between arrogance and self-belief. It's very important to recognize that difference and to respect it.

On my journey to lose weight and become an Ironman, I shared almost every aspect of my life on social media. I shared what I ate. I shared my workouts. I shared my ups and my downs. In the beginning, when I'd post about running for 20 minutes, I think most people found it great that I was trying to make a change and that I was working so hard to achieve my Dream. But as my training developed and I became more athletic, my posts became about running for 3 hours, or swimming 2 miles, or riding my bike 100 miles. At that point, it's possible that, to some people, my journey had become less about the journey and more about bragging rights.

Nothing could be further from the truth.

I shared my journey for two reasons: (1) to keep myself on track by being accountable to those who followed me, and (2) to inspire others to change their lives too. For every person who would tell me that they were tired of hearing about my workouts and my journey, I'd have ten more telling me how proud they were of what I was achieving, or even more importantly, how inspired they were.

Years ago, I wouldn't have been able to say this. I am, I like to say, a recovering egomaniac. Back before my wife and I separated, I remember one day when she gave me Rick Warren's book *The Purpose Driven Life* and she asked me to read it. I opened it up to the first page and read the first line aloud.

It's not all about you.

That was the first sentence I read.

I remember closing the book, sitting it down, looking at her, and saying, "Yes, it is."

I didn't open the book again until almost three years later. Over those three years, I separated from my wife (even though we did get back together) and lost the business that I'd run for 11 years. We lost our home and had to move almost 8 hours away from Lexington to take a job, the only job I could find.

It was a time when I lost everything that I had worked so hard to achieve. It took me losing everything to realize that all of it was really nothing. I learned humility. I learned what was truly important to me—my faith, my wife, my kids. I learned the most valuable lesson of all: in all things be humble.

So on my journey from Couch Potato to Ironman, I shared a lot of stuff. I was proud of myself for what I managed to achieve, and I still am. But believing in yourself is very different than being arrogant.

Be proud of all of the small steps you take. Be that light to others. Don't worry what others think or say. Keep your heart humble, your motives pure, and your Belief in self strong.

CHAPTER SIX
DETERMINATION

Over the last five chapters, we've talked about the Building Blocks of Success and how each one plays into the overall mission of achieving your Dream. We've discussed the Three Stages of Success as well.

Now we turn our focus to the sixth and final Building Block of Success, and the one that is the most important to success: Determination.

Mario Andretti, the famous race car driver, once said:

"Desire is the key to motivation, but it's the determination and commitment to unrelenting pursuit of your goal - a commitment to excellence - that will enable you to attain the success you seek."

We've discussed both Desire and motivation in terms of Inspiration, but like Andretti said, it's the Determination that enables you to attain success.

What is Determination?

Determination is, simply put, the quality that makes you continue trying to achieve something difficult—but let's go a little further.

First, Determination is a quality that you hold. It's not something you're born with. It's not genetic. It's a quality that you develop over time. That is essential to understand because, even if you lack Determination when you begin your journey, you can nurture and develop it over the course of your journey. That's what had to happen for me. I wanted to quit *plenty* of times on my health and fitness journey. I've told you that I even stopped running at the public park out of embarrassment when I first began, but what I didn't mention was that I almost gave up right then. Oh yeah. I wanted to quit, but somehow I didn't. I found the Determination to keep going. As the journey continued to get tougher, there were more times that I wanted to quit, but my Determination won out in the end. Over time, I honed my Determination into a skill.

Next, the quality of Determination "makes you continue trying to do or achieve something." Determination is perpetual; it's always in motion and it's goal-driven. You can't be determined if you are acting randomly, with no set goal in mind. That's why you Dream and Plan so you can Achieve. Determination allows you to continue trying to reach your goal. Your Determination will keep you from giving up.

The end result is that you achieve something you had considered "difficult." Achieving the simple doesn't take Determination; we all know that. Achieving simple things isn't all that satisfying, either. We all have an innate desire to achieve bigger, more "difficult" things. As you continue on your journey, remember that even though the end goal may seem difficult to reach, you need only stick with these Six Building Blocks to achieve the success that you Desire.

Is Determination Measurable?

Wouldn't it be nice if we could wake up every morning and jump on a scale that would tell us how high, or low, our Determination would be for that day? If we got on the scale and it read "Low," we could just crawl back in bed and save up the energy for another day. If the scale said "High," we could spend the day furiously focused, knowing that the day was not to be wasted.

Unfortunately, we don't have that luxury. Each day we have to decide to be determined, regardless of what is going on in our lives. From day to day, our level of Determination may waver from high to low, but acknowledging that it is there, and using it to move forward, is essential to achieving Success.

Whether you feel that your Determination is "low" or "high" on a particular day, there are steps that you can take to increase your level of Determination. Each day, it's important to focus on honing your Determination so that, even on the days where you may feel as though it is waning a bit, you can still come back strong and focused.

Below, we will discuss a few things that you can do for those times where your Determination meter seems to be a little on the "low" side.

Developing Determination

As the definition says, Determination is a quality. Like any other quality you possess, you develop it by using it. We aren't born as kind people, for instance; we develop kindness by working on it. It is, of course, a part of our upbringing; our parents show us kindness and we learn to show kindness to others. But if we don't practice being kind to others, we can forget how to be habitually kind to others. Determination works the same way.

Determination can be developed using the small-steps strategy we've discussed several times before. As you start out on your journey, set small goals for yourself. Do you want to lose weight? You can't lose it all in one day. You need to set those small, achievable goals for yourself. When you achieve one, set another. Once you achieve it, set another. But make each goal a little more difficult each time—there's no growth where there's no challenge.

If you want to lose 50 pounds, you might set a goal of 2 pounds in the first week. Once you lose 2 pounds in a week, try to lose 3 pounds the next week. It may be harder to do, but by setting a more difficult goal for yourself, you will be honing your Determination into a finely-tuned weapon. If you want to run a marathon, start out by conquering a 5K. Then set your sights on a 10K—and so on.

The problem with keeping your goals the same each time is that you plateau. You may do well and make major progress for the first few weeks or months, but over time, if you keep setting the same small goals, you will reach a point where they no longer get you any further. You need to push the limits of your Determination to develop greater potential.

When I began my journey to lose weight and get in shape, I started with walking. At first, I could only walk about a mile before I got tired, but I always wanted to push myself to go farther. So I did. In doing so, I was able to increase my Determination enough to decide to become a runner.

I set the goal of running a 5K. As I trained, each week I pushed myself to run longer times and longer distances. Each week, as I achieved those incremental goals, I could feel my level of Determination growing. Each event that I participated in—the 10K, the half-marathon, the marathon, the half-Ironman, and finally the Ironman—were all made possible by pushing myself to go farther each day than I did the day before. By doing so, I was able to develop my Determination into laser-like focus.

At the same time, Determination isn't just a self-made quality. While only you can control your level of Determination, it can be *influenced* by the people around you. For that reason, it's important to surround yourself with like-minded people who can help you develop your Determination.

Earlier in the book, I wrote about the trip my wife and I won to Hawaii to see the Ironman World Championship. It was just two months after my failed attempt at Ironman Louisville, so my Determination was at a very low point—as was my level of Inspiration. But while my wife and I watched these world-class athletes, not only was I inspired, but I could also feel my Determination returning. If these athletes could do it, why couldn't I?

I remember watching one of the endurance athletes whom I admire the most, Lew Hollander, swimming out to the starting point of the race. If you don't know about Lew, let me tell you a little about him. Lew is consistently one of the oldest triathletes competing at Kona. The year that I was there, he was 82 years old.

Just let that sink in for a while. *82 years old.*

He swims 2.4 miles in the ocean, then rides his bike 112 miles on one of the toughest courses in the world, and then runs 26.2 miles through the lava fields of Hawaii. All in under 17 hours. Lew is an amazing man; I had the opportunity to meet him on my trip and speak with him briefly. I told him about my weight loss journey and how I had unsuccessfully attempted Ironman Louisville. I also told him that I was struggling with staying focused on the Dream of being an Ironman.

He stopped me mid-sentence and looked me in the eyes in a grandfatherly way, and he said, "It's hard. It's tough to do. But if you really want to do it, then don't give up."

Just those few simple words were enough to re-kindle my Determination and make me realize that I could do it. I could train harder. I could push myself further. I could become an Ironman.

On the flight home from Hawaii, I read a book by Rich Roll, an incredible endurance athlete. The book, titled *Finding Ultra: Rejecting Middle Age, Becoming One of the World's Fittest Men, and Discovering Myself*, told the story of how Rich—an attorney like me—had struggled with self-esteem issues, alcohol, marital issues, and a life seemingly spiraling out of control. He then decided to make a change; he switched to a vegan lifestyle and started running. Not only did he become a runner, he became a triathlete—and he didn't just become an ordinary triathlete. Rich decided to become an ultra-triathlete.

He and a friend decided to do five Ironman distance events on the five islands of Hawaii in five days. They pushed themselves to the limits and beyond. In five days, they completed their quest. How in the world could a human being accomplish that?

It's simple: Determination. Reading Rich's story only fueled my Determination even more.

Once we returned home, I was ready to get back at it. I began taking small steps again towards my Dream of becoming an Ironman. Not only did I find my Determination spurred along by successful, world-class athletes, but my Determination was also influenced by my friends with whom I trained on a day-to-day basis.

In June of 2013, I decided to participate in a century ride in Central Kentucky as part of my Ironman training. For those of you who aren't familiar with a century ride, it is a 100-mile bike ride. Although Central Kentucky is mostly rolling hills, it does have some pretty steep climbs that can make a 100-mile ride quite an experience.

I had no intentions of riding with anyone that day, but early on during the ride, I met up with my friend Coy Martinez, who was also training for Ironman Louisville. Coy and I decided to ride together, which was a great decision. As we rode we talked about our training. We talked about the ups and downs that we'd encountered on the journey. We shared the tales of the struggles to balance family, work, and training. Having the companionship made the ride much more enjoyable, but it also helped fuel my Determination to finish the ride. There were several times that I struggled on the ride and I wanted to give up, but Coy encouraged me—not so much by speaking words of encouragement, but simply by riding there with me. And as she rode, it helped me become more and more determined to keep up with her, which I did. We finished the ride. It was a great feeling to finish, and it was a great source of fuel for my Determination to finish Ironman Louisville.

As you begin your journey, look for others who can help you develop your Determination. If your goal is weight loss, look for someone who is successful at getting fit. Surround yourself with like-minded people who can help you fuel your Determination. Find a co-worker who wants to get fit and walk together. Join a gym and find someone to do classes with. Whatever your end goal, develop your Determination with the help of others.

Determination and End Results

We live in a society where most people want the things that they want *now*. Our culture has developed a "fast-food mentality" for life in general, a mentality based on the underlying principle that, when we want something, we should be able to have it *now*. After all, that's what the fast food industry is all about; if you want a burger, there's a fast food restaurant that will give you one in just a few minutes, if not a few seconds. If you want fried chicken, go across the street to the other restaurant and you can get that instead. There's a chain for almost anything you can imagine.

And so this fast-food mentality creeps into other aspects of our daily lives. We want to lose weight, but we give up when it doesn't impress us the first week. We want a raise at work, but we get frustrated and quit when it doesn't happen after a few weeks of hard work. We want a lifetime of love and a relationship that will last forever, but we want to give up the search after a few bad dates.

We know what we want, and we want it NOW!

That's the way we tend to think. I'm guilty of it; I'm sure you are too. But, to get anywhere, we need to re-wire our minds to think long-term. You don't find success overnight, and a fast-food mentality will only leave you discouraged and defeated.

So how long will it take you to reach your end goal?

As long as it takes.

Let me say that again. *It'll take you as long as it takes.*

It's foolhardy to put a time limit on success. We want to, but most of us do it anyway. I said that I wanted to be an Ironman in August 2012. Guess what? It didn't happen. I didn't achieve my Dream in the time that I had "allotted" for myself. That was, in hindsight, a *huge* error on my part. I wasn't thinking about taking the time to make sure that I did things the best way possible. I plowed ahead, thinking over and over to myself: *I want this now. I want this now.*

Because of that fast-food mentality that I took with my Dream, I almost gave up when I couldn't realize it when I wanted. It took more Determination than ever before to get back in the saddle and make that Dream a reality. It wasn't easy, but nothing worth achieving ever is.

The only true failure is to give up. Many times you will face obstacles on your journey to success, and many times you may need to re-evaluate what you're doing to reach that end goal, but not achieving your goal when you intend is not a bad reflection on your Determination. It isn't an indication of failure. It's just one more learning experience. When we fall short of our goals, it is merely an opportunity for us to step back and find another way.

When I began training again after my unsuccessful Ironman attempt, I realized that I needed to change a few things. Over time, I realized that my problem wasn't that I lacked the Determination. It was simply that I needed to change a few things in my training routine to make sure that I could do what I needed to do.

The best thing that I did was hire my coach, Beth Atnip. I also joined a Masters swim team where I received coaching from Susan Bradley Cox, an incredible woman in the International Triathlete Hall of Fame.

Both Beth and Susan provided me with workouts each day, which really fed into my small-steps mindset. Each week, as the workouts ramped up, I pushed myself further and harder. As I finished more and more difficult workouts, my Determination sharpened.

In the final month of training, I was putting in over 20 hours a week working out. I was swimming, biking, and running in almost every spare moment I had. Sure enough, that Determination carried over to race day and helped me cross the finish line.

I made it through the swim 45 minutes faster than I had the year before. What was even more incredible to me was that I felt *less* tired after the swim than I had the year before. (I definitely owe that *huge* improvement on the swim to Susan's coaching.)

After the swim I jumped on the bike and felt really good. I finished the biking in just over 7 hours and knew that I had plenty of time to make it through the run. When I hit the run course I still felt pretty good, but within three miles I noticed that I was drifting to my left as I ran. I started feeling very dizzy. That's when I knew there was a big problem.

I made it to a rest station and sat down on the sidewalk. A volunteer came over and asked me if she could get anything for me. I asked for some water and ice. Every few minutes she would come back to check on me and each time I'd ask for more ice. I had overheated. I was in danger of falling out of the race again because of it.

I was wearing a tracking device during the race so my wife could follow me throughout the day and see where I was on the course. I knew that she could see my little dot just sitting there, frozen, not going anywhere. I knew she was with a lot of our friends and family, and I knew that they were continually asking her "Where is he now?"

All I could think about was how it would feel to *DNF* (Did Not Finish) again. I couldn't bear the thought of facing all those people who had come to see me complete the race this year. I thought about all of the training that I'd been through, all of the time, effort, and money that I had sacrificed. But mostly, I thought about my wife. I knew she wouldn't be disappointed in me, but I wanted to do this for her as much as I did for myself.

So I stood up. I regained my balance and my bearings and I started doing the Ironman math. It's amazing how your mind starts to work during an endurance event—you're constantly doing math. For me, knowing that my biggest competition was the 17-hour time limit, I was continuously doing math. Since I knew I would have to walk the remaining 23.2 miles of the marathon, my mind began to calculate: how fast do I have to walk to finish on time?

I set out walking as fast as I could. With each mile, my Determination grew within me. It was the small-steps philosophy applied to its fullest and most literal. With each passing mile, I knew I was closer to reaching my goal. Even as my feet began to bleed from blisters and my thighs began to burn from rubbing raw, I knew that I would finish if I could just keep my pace.

Volunteers cheered me on. Other athletes cheered me on. Friends on the course cheered me on. I was beginning to understand that this was really going to happen. *I was going to be an Ironman.* As I rounded the last turn, I could see the lights at the finish line at Fourth Street Live in downtown Louisville. I could hear the music blaring. I could hear the announcer saying "*YOU are an Ironman!*" as other competitors crossed the line. I could hear the roar of the crowd. Yes, a *roar*, at 11:30 at night—16 and a half hours after the event began, there were still thousands of people waiting at the finish line cheering us all on.

I completely lost it. I broke down in tears. I hung my head for a few moments as the realization began to sink in.

I did it, I thought. *I'm gonna be an Ironman.*

I looked up and there was my coach, Beth, running toward me. She hugged me and cheered me and told me to go finish the race. Walking across the finish line was one of the most amazing moments of my life.

CONCLUSION

I'm not sure where you are in your life. I'm not sure what issues you face. But I am certain that you and I are alike. You feel—and wish—that you could have done certain things differently in life. There are things that you would still like to change, to improve about your life. There are Dreams you want to realize and a person, a version of yourself, that you've always wanted to be. I know those feelings. I have walked a mile (or more) in your shoes.

The good news is that you've now read this book, and you have the principles to help you achieve the success you're after. You know the Six Building Blocks of Success; you know how to nurture them, how to let them guide you to focus your Dream and begin taking steps to a new reality. I know that if I can do it, so can you.

I'll never forget waking up that June morning in 2014. The air outside was already hot and humid, and the air inside the condo was full of excitement as we prepared to head to Dollywood. It had been four years since the embarrassing moment on the roller coaster that had become the turning point for my life.

"Is everybody ready to go?", I yelled out through the halls.

No reply. Typical of teenagers.

I made my way to my son's room. "Mason, are you ready to go?" I asked.

"Yes," he replied.

I made my way across the hall to Abby's room. "Abby, are you ready to go?"

"Yes," she mumbled from behind the screen of her iPhone.

"Okay gang. Let's go!" I said enthusiastically. On the inside, though, I was a bit apprehensive. I hadn't been on a roller coaster since that failed attempt—would I fit? Would I disappoint my daughter (and myself) again?

The rest of the morning played out just as it had four years before. We arrived at the park early and waited. When they opened the gates, we were off to the Thunderhead—but this time I wasn't winded on the walk to the ride. I didn't have to stop every 20 feet on the uphill climb to catch my breath. I was excited! I was ready to do this!

This time when we got to the coaster, we were at the front of the line. Again, we headed to the very back car. When the gate opened, we jumped in the car as fast as we could.

Seat belt fastened—check. *Now the reality check.* I reached up and grabbed the safety bar. (I think I even said a little prayer under my breath.) I pulled the bar down slowly. It kept coming down lower, and lower, and lower, and then—*click.*

I did it! I fit on the ride! And there was *plenty* of room left over between me and the bar, where there hadn't been enough room four years before.

The coaster kicked into gear and we emerged from the wooden enclosure. We slowly ratcheted up the wooden mountain in front of us, the clanking of the chains like a mechanical metronome humming a tuneless song to itself.

Once we reached the top . . . we were off! The car rocked and rolled on the wooden track, up and down, around and around. I held on for dear life while my daughter threw her hands in the air and screamed at the top of her lungs.

Oh, what the hell, I thought. I shot my hands up into the air, closed my eyes, and screamed as loud as my daughter.

After it was over, we coasted back into the tight wooden enclosure where we had started our journey just moments before.

As the cars came to a stop my daughter smiled and looked at me. She said, "That was awesome, Dad."

"Yes it was, sweetheart," I said, trying not to cry. The emotions of the journey I'd been on for the past four years started to well up inside of me.

"Yes, it was."

I *almost* missed this moment. I *almost* missed having the chance to do this. There were times where I wanted to give up on my journey, times when I didn't know for sure if I could make it.

But I did.

Don't miss *your* moment. Use this book as a resource to make those changes so you can live your moment. You've already taken that first small step reading this book.

Now what small step will you take **tomorrow?**

Mark's "Before" Picture (with his wife, Annita)
386+ pounds

Mark's First 5K @ the Great Buffalo Chase
Frankfort, Kentucky — July 4, 2011

Mark's First Half Marathon @ The Iron Horse Half Marathon
Midway, Kentucky — October 23, 2011

Mark @ Ironman Louisville
Louisville, Kentucky — August 25, 2013

Mark riding "the Slingshot" with his daughter Abby
Pigeon Forge, Tennessee — June 2014

www.ingramcontent.com/pod-product-compliance
Lightning Source LLC
Chambersburg PA
CBHW050604300426
44112CB00013B/2068